Better Homes and Gardens®

Quick Breads
Cook Book

© Meredith Corporation, 1975. All Rights Reserved.
Printed in the United States of America. First Edition. First Printing.
Library of Congress Catalog Card Number: 74-79985
SBN: 696-00800-9

On the cover: Slice up a loaf of flavor-packed *Granola-Prune Bread* for a luncheon treat. Or, pass zippy *Mexican Muffins,* dotted with corn, chili peppers, and pimiento for dinner.

Above: This colorful quick bread assortment includes *Peppy Pepper Muffins,* jam-dotted *Daisy Biscuits,* and iced *Fruit-Filled Coffee Cake.* (See Index for page numbers.)

Contents

BETTER HOMES AND GARDENS BOOKS

Editorial Director: Don Dooley
Managing Editor: Malcolm E. Robinson   Art Director: John Berg
Asst. Managing Editor: Lawrence D. Clayton   Asst. Art Director: Randall Yontz
Food Editor: Nancy Morton
Senior Food Editor: Joyce Trollope
Associate Editors: Sharyl Heiken, Rosemary C. Hutchinson, Elizabeth Strait
Assistant Editors: Sandra Granseth, Catherine Penney
Designers: Harijs Priekulis, Faith Berven
Contributing Editor: Pat Olson

Our seal assures you that every recipe in the *Quick Breads Cook Book* is endorsed by the Better Homes and Gardens Test Kitchen. Each recipe is thoroughly tested for family appeal, practicality, and deliciousness.

Fun with Quick Breads

Have you ever started browsing through a book and found that you just couldn't put it down? You're reading one of those books now. From beginning to end, you'll find quick ways to add a homemade touch to your meals — something that homemakers strive for.

With the *Quick Breads Cook Book* at your fingertips, you, too, can enjoy the satisfaction of tumbling a batch of hot homemade muffins into a basket; setting a bowl of whipped butter and honey on the table with your perfect, flaky biscuits; or serving glazed doughnuts or that show-stopping coffee cake.

It's easy to understand why quick breads are so popular. First of all, there is such a wide variety of taste-tempting breads from which to choose. And secondly, they are relatively speedy to prepare and bake, especially when you take into account the rising time necessary for yeast bread preparation.

Although biscuits, muffins, and nut breads play a particularly tasty role in rounding out the meal, the quick bread family is not limited to the bread and butter plate. In fact, feathery pancakes and crisp waffles are served as main dishes. And, doughnuts often star as the meal-ending dessert.

◀ **These delectable natural treats** offer wholesome, nutritious eating. You will agree when you try *Wheat Germ Corn Bread, Sunflower-Whole Wheat Muffins,* and *Buttermilk-Bran Scones.* (See Index for page numbers.)

Quick breads can be as similar as two muffins sparked with either orange or cranberry, or as varied as herbed dumplings crowning a bubbling stew, or chocolate-flavored doughnuts. That's why it's important to familiarize yourself with the various types of doughs, batters, ingredients, and preparation techniques common to the wide selection of quick breads.

Types of Quick Breads

There are two types of quick breads in this book. The first type includes those leavened with baking powder, soda, or steam. You bake or fry the mixture immediately after mixing. The other group of recipes gets a head start with convenience products, such as refrigerated biscuits, hot roll mix, and frozen bread dough.

The first group can be categorized also according to the consistency of the batter or dough. Pour batters, drop batters, and soft doughs are the three standard quick bread mixtures. Pour batters have the highest proportion of liquid to flour and are used to make stacks of fluffy pancakes and hearty waffles. Drop batters contain proportionately less liquid and are made into muffins, drop biscuits, dumplings, fruit and nut loaves, and some coffee cakes. Soft doughs are stiff enough to be patted, rolled, shaped, or cut into biscuits, scones, or doughnuts.

Quick Bread Ingredients

An astonishing array of breads start with the same basic ingredients. Of course, not all of the following will be found in every quick bread recipe, just as you will find others not listed.

Flour is the major ingredient. It contains gluten, which forms the framework that gives bread its structure. All-purpose flour, made from a blend of hard- and soft-wheat flours, has the most gluten of household flours and is most commonly used. However, specialty flours, such as whole wheat and rye, add interesting flavor and texture to bread. In most cases, you'll have to use these specialty flours in combination with all-purpose flour to ensure enough gluten.

Self-rising flour is another type that you can use successfully in most quick breads. It is an all-purpose flour to which baking powder and salt have been added. When substituting self-rising flour for the regular all-purpose flour, be sure to omit an appropriate amount of leavener and salt. One cup of self-rising flour contains the equivalent of 1½ teaspoons baking powder and ½ teaspoon salt.

Leavening agents give the distinctive lightness to quick breads. Baking powder, baking soda, and steam, used either separately or in combination, allow the dough to expand during baking, giving volume to the product.

Sugar adds flavor, aids in browning, and increases tenderness. Coffee cakes and nut loaves contain a higher proportion of sugar than biscuits and muffins.

Shortening or fats used in making quick breads include butter, margarine, vegetable shortenings, and cooking oil. The function of shortening is threefold: it adds tenderness and flavor, and aids in browning. Cooled, melted shortening and cooking oil may be used interchangeably.

Liquids used in making quick breads add moisture and oftentimes nutrition. Commonly used liquids include milk, water, and fruit juices.

Salt is used primarily for flavor.

Measuring Ingredients

Accurate measurements are very important to the finished product. To begin with, use standard measuring utensils suitable for dry and liquid measuring. Do not pour or level ingredients over a mixing bowl of measured ingredients.

It is not necessary to sift all-purpose flour for making quick breads. However, be sure to stir the flour in the canister before spooning it lightly into the measuring cup. Level off the cup with a straight edge spatula. Do not pack or shake flour down in the cup.

Some ingredients do need to be packed for accurate measuring. One of these is brown sugar. Firmly pack the sugar into the measuring cup so that it will retain the cup's shape when turned out. Another ingredient that requires packing is vegetable shortening.

Measure liquids in a glass measuring cup that has a rim above the last measuring mark. With the cup sitting on a flat, level surface, pour the liquid in, and read the measuring mark at eye level.

Baking Containers and Tips

Use the size and type container called for in the recipe for best results of the baked product. Whenever a *baking pan* is called for in the recipe, use a metal container. However, use a glass container when a *baking dish* is specified. Foods baked in glass baking dishes require lower baking temperatures than those baked in metal containers. Reduce the oven temperature by 25° when substituting a glass container for a metal pan.

If you are placing more than one pan in the oven at the same time, be sure to stagger the pans on the oven racks so that air will circulate freely in the oven and bake the breads evenly.

Allow many quick breads, such as coffee cakes and loaves, to cool in pans about 10 minutes before removing from the pan. They will come out more easily and remain intact. Complete the cooling on a wire rack.

Nutritional Value

Bread plays an important part in a balanced diet. Along with cereal and pasta, breads make up one of the basic four food groups. The daily requirement from this group is four or more servings.

Use only flours that have been enriched with iron and the B vitamins. Other ingredients used in quick breads, such as milk, eggs, and fat, also contribute to the nutritious diet. In addition, breads contain a small amount of protein. When served with milk, they make a valuable dietary contribution.

Quick Breads at High Altitudes

Quick breads are not greatly affected by high altitudes, since they are not as delicate as cakes. However, if you are having difficulty with baking at high altitudes, you will have to experiment by using slightly less baking powder and a little more liquid.

Storage Tips

Most quick breads are at their best when served hot from the oven. However, if necessary, store them for a short period of time in a cool, dry place. Wrap them tightly in foil or clear plastic wrap or place them in a plastic bag. Reheating will enhance the flavor of many leftover breads.

Freeze quick breads tightly wrapped in moisture-vaporproof wrap. Thaw foil-wrapped biscuits on a baking sheet in a 250° to 300° oven about 20 minutes. Thaw wrapped muffins at room temperature for 1 hour or foil-wrapped at 250° to 300° till hot.

QUICK BREAD MIX

Use to make specially marked recipes—

In large bowl thoroughly stir together 10 cups all-purpose flour, ⅓ cup baking powder, ¼ cup sugar, and 1 tablespoon salt; mix well. Cut 2 cups shortening that does not require refrigeration into dry ingredients till mixture resembles coarse cornmeal. Store in tightly covered container up to 6 weeks at room temperature. Freeze for longer storage.

To measure, spoon mix into measuring cup; level with spatula. Makes 12 cups.

Memorable Coffee Cakes and Loaves

Steaming coffee...congenial friends...a morning or afternoon of friendly conversation...and a mouth-watering, jam-filled coffee cake...that's what this section is all about. Friends and family won't need much coaxing to have second servings of these tasty coffee-time treats.

Make a plain or fancy, quick or more involved coffee cake as your mood dictates. Consider a fragrant, spiced coffee cake drizzled with glistening icing to welcome a new neighbor. Or, let your kids pull apart some fresh-baked sweet rolls for a lip-smacking snack.

Nut breads and loaves are superb meal-mates. Bake them up the day before, then thinly slice the loaf, and spread slices lightly with butter or margarine.

For a delectable partner to serve with whipped cream-topped spiced tea or coffee, try *Apple Dandy Rolls, Gumdrop Bread,* or *Cherry Coffee Cake.* This quick bread trio is sure to please your guests. (See Index for page numbers.)

Coffee-Time Pleasers

Double-Deck Orange Coffee Cake

2½ cups packaged biscuit mix *or*
 Quick Bread Mix (see page 7)
 3 tablespoons sugar
 1 beaten egg
 ½ cup milk
 Orange Filling
 Orange Glaze

Stir mix and sugar together. Add egg and milk; stir till blended. Knead on lightly floured surface (8 to 10 strokes). Divide dough in 2 *almost-equal parts*. Roll larger part to 8-inch circle; place in greased 9-inch pie plate, patting dough ½ inch up sides. Sprinkle with filling. Roll remaining dough to 7-inch circle; place atop filling. With scissors, snip 1-inch slashes around edge of top layer. Bake at 375° for 25 to 30 minutes. Remove from pie plate. Drizzle with glaze. Trim with shredded orange peel if desired. Serve warm. Serves 10 to 12.

Orange Filling: Mix ⅓ cup packed brown sugar; ⅓ cup chopped walnuts; 2 tablespoons all-purpose flour; 2 tablespoons butter, melted; and 1 tablespoon grated orange peel.

Orange Glaze: Add enough orange juice (1 to 1½ tablespoons) to ¾ cup sifted powdered sugar to make of drizzling consistency.

Cinnamon-Raisin Coffee Cake

2½ cups packaged biscuit mix *or*
 Quick Bread Mix (see page 7)
 2 tablespoons granulated sugar
 ½ teaspoon ground cinnamon
 2 beaten eggs
 ¾ cup milk
 ½ cup raisins
 ⅓ cup chopped walnuts
 ⅓ cup packed brown sugar
 2 tablespoons butter, softened

Mix first 3 ingredients. Add eggs and milk; stir till moistened. Stir in raisins. Turn into greased 11x7½x1½-inch baking pan. Combine remaining ingredients; sprinkle atop. Bake at 375° for 20 to 25 minutes. Serves 12.

Blueberry Coffee Cake

Generous blueberry pie filling makes this one good enough for a dessert. Next time substitute apple or cherry pie filling instead.

1¼ cups all-purpose flour
 ½ cup sugar
 1 teaspoon baking powder
 ¼ teaspoon baking soda
 ¼ teaspoon salt
 • • •
 1 beaten egg
 ½ cup butter *or* margarine, melted
 ½ cup buttermilk
 1 teaspoon vanilla
 • • •
 ½ cup all-purpose flour
 ¼ cup sugar
 2 tablespoons butter *or*
 margarine, softened
 • • •
 ½ teaspoon grated lemon peel
 1 21-ounce can blueberry pie filling

In mixing bowl thoroughly stir together the 1¼ cups all-purpose flour, ½ cup sugar, baking powder, baking soda, and salt. Combine egg, ½ cup melted butter or margarine, buttermilk, and vanilla. Add to dry ingredients, mixing well. Turn batter into greased and floured 9x9 x2-inch baking pan.

In small mixing bowl combine ½ cup all-purpose flour, ¼ cup sugar, and 2 tablespoons softened butter or margarine till mixture is crumbly. Sprinkle *half* of the crumb mixture atop batter in pan. Stir grated lemon peel into blueberry pie filling; spread filling over crumb layer. Sprinkle top with remaining crumbs. Bake at 350° till done, 40 to 45 minutes. Serve coffee cake while warm. Makes 8 or 9 servings.

Double your eating pleasure with sunny *Double-Deck Orange Coffee Cake.* Mouth-watering orange filling and delicious orange glaze make this a special coffee cake you'll enjoy serving to the family or favorite neighbors. ▶

Strawberry Swirl Squares

⅔ cup shortening
⅔ cup sugar
2 cups all-purpose flour
2 teaspoons baking powder
½ teaspoon salt
½ teaspoon baking soda
½ teaspoon ground nutmeg
2 beaten eggs
⅔ cup buttermilk
½ cup strawberry preserves
¼ cup chopped walnuts

Cream shortening and sugar together well. Stir together flour, baking powder, salt, soda, and nutmeg; add to creamed mixture, mixing well. Reserve ½ cup for topping. Combine eggs and buttermilk; add to remaining flour mixture, stirring just till mixed. Spread in greased 9x9x2-inch baking pan. Cut up large pieces of berries in preserves; drop by spoonfuls atop batter. Swirl spatula through batter to marble. Stir nuts into reserved ½ cup crumb mixture; sprinkle atop batter. Bake at 375° about 30 minutes. Makes 8 or 9 servings.

Best Banana Coffee Cake

½ cup butter *or* margarine
¾ cup sugar
1¾ cups all-purpose flour
2 teaspoons baking powder
½ teaspoon salt
½ teaspoon ground cinnamon
¼ teaspoon baking soda
2 beaten eggs
2 ripe medium bananas, mashed
    (1 cup)
¼ cup milk
1 teaspoon vanilla

In bowl cream butter and sugar together well. Add ¾ *cup* of the flour; stir just till mixture resembles coarse crumbs. Reserve ½ cup for topping. Stir together remaining 1 cup flour, baking powder, salt, cinnamon, and soda. Stir into butter mixture. Combine eggs, mashed banana, milk, and vanilla. Add to dry ingredients, stirring just till mixed. Spread in greased 9x9x2-inch baking pan. Sprinkle with the reserved ½ cup crumb mixture. Bake at 375° for 25 to 30 minutes. Makes 9 servings.

Cream sugar and shortening to a fluffy consistency by rubbing the mixture against the side of a bowl with the back of a wooden spoon. Or, cream with an electric mixer. Creaming the shortening alone or with sugar incorporates air to give products a light, cake-like texture.

Cowboy Coffee Cake

2½ cups all-purpose flour
2 cups packed brown sugar
½ teaspoon salt
⅔ cup shortening
2 teaspoons baking powder
½ teaspoon baking soda
½ teaspoon ground cinnamon
½ teaspoon ground nutmeg
1 cup sour milk
2 beaten eggs

In bowl mix flour, sugar, and salt. Cut in shortening till mixture resembles coarse crumbs; reserve ½ cup for topping. To remaining crumbs add baking powder, soda, and spices; mix well. Add milk and eggs; mix well. Turn into 2 greased and floured 8x1½-inch round baking pans; top with the ½ cup reserved crumbs. Bake at 375° for 25 to 30 minutes. Serve warm. Makes 2 coffee cakes, 6 to 8 servings each.

Franciscan Coffee Cake

    ½ cup butter *or* margarine
    1 cup granulated sugar
    1 egg
    1½ cups all-purpose flour
    2 teaspoons baking powder
    ½ cup milk
    1 cup chopped peeled apple
    ¾ cup chopped dried figs
    ½ cup packed brown sugar
    ½ teaspoon ground cinnamon
    2 tablespoons butter *or* margarine
    ½ cup chopped walnuts

In bowl cream butter and granulated sugar to-gether well. Beat in egg. Thoroughly stir together flour, baking powder, and ½ teaspoon salt. Stir into creamed mixture alternately with milk. Fold in apple and figs. Turn into greased and floured 9x9x2-inch baking pan. Combine brown sugar and cinnamon; cut in 2 table-spoons butter till crumbly. Stir in nuts. Sprinkle crumbly mixture over batter. Bake at 350° about 45 minutes. Serves 8 or 9.

Fruit-Filled Coffee Cake

Ladder-style coffee cake shown on page 2—

    1 3-ounce package cream cheese
    ¼ cup butter *or* margarine
    2 cups Quick Bread Mix
        (see page 7)
    ¼ cup milk
    ¼ cup chopped pecans
    ½ of a 12-ounce can cherry *or* apricot
        cake and pastry filling
        Confectioners' Icing

In bowl cut cream cheese and butter into Quick Bread Mix till crumbly. Add milk and nuts; mix well. Knead on lightly floured sur-face (8 to 10 strokes). Roll dough to 12x8-inch rectangle on waxed paper. Turn onto greased baking sheet; remove paper. Spread filling lengthwise down center one-third of dough. Make 2½-inch cuts at 1-inch intervals on both long sides. Fold strips over filling. Bake at 425° till done, about 15 minutes. Drizzle with Con-fectioners' Icing while warm. Serves 6 to 8.

Confectioners' Icing: Mix ½ cup powdered sugar, ¼ teaspoon vanilla, and enough milk till of drizzling consistency (about 1 tablespoon).

Gingerbread Coffee Cake

    2 14-ounce packages gingerbread
        mix
    2 cups dairy sour cream
    4 eggs
    ⅔ cup water
    1½ teaspoons grated orange peel
    ½ cup sugar
    ¼ cup orange juice
    1 teaspoon lemon juice

Combine mix, sour cream, eggs, water, and orange peel. Beat at low speed of electric mixer till moistened, scraping bowl. Beat 3 minutes at medium speed till smooth. Turn into well-greased 10-inch fluted tube pan. Bake at 350° for 55 to 60 minutes. Cool 10 min-utes. Remove from pan. Using long-tined fork or skewer, punch holes in top of coffee cake at 1-inch intervals. In saucepan combine sugar, orange juice, and lemon juice; bring to boil. Brush over coffee cake, allowing cake to ab-sorb sauce. Serves 16.

Lemon Coffee Cake

    1 package 2-layer-size lemon
        cake mix
    ¼ cup all-purpose flour
    ¼ cup sugar
    1½ teaspoons ground nutmeg
    1 teaspoon grated lemon peel
    3 tablespoons butter *or* margarine
    1 3¾- or 3⅝-ounce package *instant*
        lemon pudding mix
    1 cup dairy sour cream
    4 eggs
    ½ cup cooking oil
    ½ cup dried currants

Remove ½ *cup* dry cake mix; combine with next 4 ingredients. Cut in butter till crumbly; set aside. In mixer bowl combine remaining cake mix, dry pudding mix, sour cream, eggs, and cooking oil. Beat 5 minutes at medium speed on electric mixer. Fold in currants. Turn *half* the batter into a greased 10-inch tube pan. Sprinkle *half* the crumb mixture atop batter. Pour remaining batter over crumb mixture; sprinkle remaining crumb mixture over top. Bake at 350° for 40 to 45 minutes. Cool in pan 10 minutes; remove from pan. Cool. Serves 16.

Cocoa Ring

1½ cups all-purpose flour
1 cup sugar
2 tablespoons unsweetened cocoa
    powder
1 teaspoon baking soda
½ teaspoon salt
½ teaspoon ground cinnamon
½ teaspoon ground nutmeg
½ teaspoon ground allspice
1 8½-ounce can applesauce
½ cup buttermilk
6 tablespoons butter, melted
1 cup chopped pecans
½ cup raisins
    Sifted powdered sugar
    Whipped Butter

In large mixing bowl thoroughly stir together flour, sugar, cocoa powder, soda, salt, and spices. Combine applesauce, buttermilk, and melted butter. Add to dry ingredients, stirring just till moistened. Fold in nuts and raisins. Turn into greased and floured 6½-cup ring mold. Bake at 325° till done, 50 to 55 minutes. Cool 10 minutes in pan on wire rack; remove from pan. Dust with powdered sugar. Serve with Whipped Butter. Makes 12 servings.

Whipped Butter: With electric mixer whip soft butter till fluffy. Dust with ground nutmeg.

Granola Squares

In small mixing bowl cream 3 tablespoons butter *or* margarine and ½ cup packed brown sugar together well. Beat in 1 egg. Add ½ cup buttermilk; mix well. Thoroughly stir together 1 cup all-purpose flour, ½ teaspoon baking soda, ¼ teaspoon salt, and ¼ teaspoon ground cinnamon; add to creamed mixture, mixing well. Fold in ⅓ cup granola cereal. Turn into greased 8x8x2-inch baking pan. Sprinkle batter with an additional ⅓ cup granola cereal. Bake at 350° for 30 to 35 minutes. Cut in squares. Serve warm or cooled. Serves 9.

◀ **Let the aroma of freshly baked** *Sour Cream-Currant Coffee Cake,* pretty *Spiced Apple Revel Loaf* (see recipe, page 23), or powdered sugar-dusted *Cocoa Ring* fill your house.

Sour Cream-Currant Coffee Cake

¾ cup dried currants
½ cup packed brown sugar
½ cup chopped walnuts
1 teaspoon ground cinnamon
1 package 2-layer-size yellow
    cake mix
4 eggs
1 cup dairy sour cream
2 tablespoons butter, melted

Mix currants, brown sugar, walnuts, and cinnamon; set aside. In large mixer bowl combine cake mix, eggs, and sour cream. Beat at low speed with electric mixer till moistened. Beat 5 minutes at medium speed, scraping bowl often. Grease and flour a 10-inch fluted tube pan. Pour melted butter in bottom of pan. Sprinkle *one-fourth* of the currant mixture in bottom of pan. Pour *half* the batter over. Cover with remaining currant mixture. Top with remaining batter. Bake at 350° for 35 to 40 minutes. Cool in pan 5 minutes; unmold carefully on rack. Cool. Makes 12 servings.

Cherry Coffee Cake

This coffee cake is shown on pages 8 and 9—

1¾ cups all-purpose flour
½ cup granulated sugar
1½ teaspoons baking powder
¼ cup butter *or* margarine
1 beaten egg
3 tablespoons milk
1 teaspoon vanilla
1 21-ounce can cherry pie filling
¼ cup packed brown sugar
½ teaspoon ground cinnamon
¼ cup butter *or* margarine

In mixing bowl thoroughly stir together *1¼ cups* of the flour, granulated sugar, baking powder, and ¼ teaspoon salt. Cut in ¼ cup butter till mixture resembles coarse crumbs. Combine egg, milk, and vanilla. Add to dry ingredients, stirring well. Spread in greased 11x7½x1½-inch baking pan. Spoon pie filling over top. Combine remaining ½ cup flour, brown sugar, and cinnamon. Cut in ¼ cup butter till mixture resembles coarse crumbs; sprinkle over all. Bake at 350° for 45 to 50 minutes. Makes 10 to 12 servings.

Chunky Apple Coffee Cake

½ cup butter *or* margarine,
  softened
½ cup sugar
1¾ cups all-purpose flour
2 beaten eggs
1 teaspoon vanilla
1½ teaspoons baking powder
½ teaspoon baking soda
1 cup chunk-style applesauce
¼ cup chopped nuts
½ teaspoon ground cinnamon

In bowl cream butter and sugar together well. Add ¾ *cup* of the flour; stir till crumbly. Reserve ½ cup. To remaining crumb mixture add eggs and vanilla; beat till smooth. Thoroughly stir together remaining 1 cup flour, baking powder, soda, and ½ teaspoon salt. Add alternately with applesauce to creamed mixture, beating after each addition. Turn into greased 10-inch pie plate. Stir nuts and cinnamon into reserved ½ cup crumb mixture; sprinkle over batter in pan. Bake at 375° for 30 to 35 minutes. Cut into wedges. Makes 10 servings.

Peanut Butter Coffee Cake

½ cup packed brown sugar
½ cup all-purpose flour
¼ cup peanut butter
2 tablespoons butter, melted
½ cup peanut butter
¼ cup shortening
1 cup packed brown sugar
2 eggs
2 cups all-purpose flour
2 teaspoons baking powder
½ teaspoon baking soda
½ teaspoon salt
1 cup milk

Mix first 4 ingredients till crumbly; set aside. Cream ½ cup peanut butter and shortening together well. Slowly beat in 1 cup brown sugar. Add eggs, one at a time, beating till fluffy. Thoroughly stir together the flour, baking powder, soda, and salt. Add alternately with milk to creamed mixture, beating after each addition. Spread in greased 13x9x2-inch baking pan. Top with crumbly mixture. Bake at 375° for 30 to 35 minutes. Serves 16 to 18.

Basic Coffee Cake

2 cups Quick Bread Mix
  (see page 7)
¼ cup granulated sugar
1 beaten egg
⅔ cup milk
2 tablespoons shortening
¼ cup packed brown sugar
2 tablespoons Quick Bread Mix
  (see page 7)
1 tablespoon butter, melted
¼ teaspoon ground cinnamon

In bowl combine first 2 ingredients. Add egg, milk, and shortening. Beat with electric mixer till smooth. Spread in greased 8x8x2-inch baking pan. Combine remaining ingredients; mix well. Sprinkle atop batter. Bake at 375° for 25 to 30 minutes. Serve warm. Serves 9.

Spicy Marble Coffee Cake: Prepare batter for Basic Coffee Cake. Divide batter in half. To *one half,* add 2 tablespoons light molasses, ½ teaspoon ground cinnamon, ¼ teaspoon ground nutmeg, and ⅛ teaspoon ground cloves. In a greased 8x8x2-inch baking pan, drop plain batter by teaspoons checkerboard fashion. Fill empty spaces with spiced batter. Swirl batters to marble. Add topping and bake as in Basic Coffee Cake.

Quick Sally Lunn

2 cups all-purpose flour
⅓ cup granulated sugar
1 tablespoon baking powder
2 beaten eggs
¾ cup milk
½ cup cooking oil
¼ cup packed brown sugar
½ teaspoon ground cinnamon, *or* ground
  cardamom *or* aniseed, crushed

In mixing bowl thoroughly stir together first 3 ingredients and ½ teaspoon salt; make a well in center. Combine eggs, milk, and oil. Pour liquid ingredients into well in dry ingredients; stir just till moistened. Pour into greased 9x9x2-inch baking pan. Combine brown sugar and spice; sprinkle atop batter. Bake at 400° for 20 to 25 minutes. Serve hot with whipped butter or cream cheese, if desired. Serves 9.

Biscuit Bubble Ring

>   1 3-ounce package cream cheese,
>   chilled
>   2 cups all-purpose flour
>   2 tablespoons granulated sugar
>   4 teaspoons baking powder
>   ½ teaspoon salt
>   ⅓ cup shortening
>   ⅔ cup milk
>   • • •
>   ¼ cup granulated sugar
>   ½ teaspoon ground cinnamon
>   • • •
>   5 tablespoons butter *or* margarine,
>   melted
>   ⅓ cup chopped pecans
>   • • •
>   ¼ cup light corn syrup
>   2 tablespoons packed brown sugar
>   2 tablespoons butter *or* margarine

There's a surprise filling in each portion of *Biscuit Bubble Ring.* You'll find cream cheese and cinnamon-sugar tucked inside each biscuit.

Cut cream cheese into 20 pieces. Shape each into a ball; set aside. Stir together the flour, 2 tablespoons granulated sugar, baking powder, and salt. Cut in shortening till mixture resembles coarse crumbs. Make a well in center of dry ingredients; add milk all at once. Stir just till dough clings together. Knead the dough gently on a lightly floured surface (10 to 12 strokes). Divide the dough into 20 pieces. Pat each piece of dough to a 2½- to 3-inch round.

Combine the ¼ cup granulated sugar and cinnamon. Place a cream cheese ball and ¼ teaspoon cinnamon-sugar mixture on *each* dough round; bring up edges of dough and pinch to seal. Pour *3 tablespoons* of the melted butter into the bottom of a 5½-cup ring mold; turn mold to coat sides. Sprinkle *half* the nuts and *half* the remaining cinnamon-sugar mixture into the mold. Roll filled biscuits in remaining melted butter. Place *half* the biscuits atop mixture in mold, seam side up. Repeat layers using the remaining pecans, cinnamon-sugar mixture, and biscuit balls.

Bake coffee cake at 375° till browned, about 25 minutes. Cool 5 minutes in pan; invert pan onto serving plate and remove pan.

Meanwhile, in small saucepan combine the corn syrup, brown sugar, and 2 tablespoons butter or margarine. Heat until sugar is melted, stirring constantly. Drizzle mixture over warm coffee cake. Makes 10 servings.

Quick Honey-Lemon Coffee Cake

>   ¼ cup honey
>   3 tablespoons butter, melted
>   1 tablespoon light corn syrup
>   2 teaspoons grated lemon peel
>   1 tablespoon lemon juice
>   2 cups packaged biscuit mix *or*
>   Quick Bread Mix (see page 7)
>   2 tablespoons sugar
>   1 beaten egg
>   ½ cup milk

Mix honey, butter, corn syrup, *1 teaspoon* of the peel, and lemon juice. Pour into well-greased 8x8x2-inch baking pan. Stir together biscuit mix, sugar, and remaining lemon peel. Combine egg and milk; stir into dry ingredients till moistened. Drop by spoonfuls over honey mixture. Bake at 375° for 20 to 25 minutes. Invert on serving plate. Serves 8 or 9.

Cranberry Relish Coffee Cake

In bowl stir together 1 cup all-purpose flour, ¼ cup sugar, 1½ teaspoons baking powder, and ½ teaspoon salt. Cut in ¼ cup shortening till mixture resembles coarse crumbs. Combine 1 beaten egg and ⅓ cup milk. Add to dry ingredients, stirring just till moistened. Spread in greased 8x8x2-inch baking pan.

Combine ½ cup cranberry-orange relish and 2 tablespoons sugar; spoon over batter. Mix ¼ cup sugar and ¼ cup all-purpose flour; cut in 2 tablespoons butter till crumbly. Sprinkle atop coffee cake. Bake at 400° for 30 to 35 minutes. Serve warm. Makes 8 or 9 servings.

Apricot Crescent

    Apricot Filling
  2 cups all-purpose flour
  1 tablespoon sugar
  1 tablespoon baking powder
  ¼ cup shortening
  2 eggs
    Milk
  1 tablespoon butter, melted
  1 tablespoon sugar
  ¼ teaspoon ground cinnamon

Apricot Filling: Combine 1 cup chopped dried apricots, ¾ cup water, ½ cup sugar, and ¼ cup chopped mixed candied fruits and peels. Bring to boil; boil till thick, about 10 minutes, stirring frequently. Mix in ¼ cup chopped walnuts. Set aside to cool.

Stir together flour, 1 tablespoon sugar, baking powder, and 1 teaspoon salt. Cut in shortening till mixture is crumbly. Separate 1 egg; set white aside. Beat together yolk and remaining whole egg; add enough milk to make ⅔ cup. Add to dry ingredients, stirring just till moistened. Knead on lightly floured surface (8 to 10 strokes). Roll dough to 16x8-inch rectangle. Brush with butter. Spread with Apricot Filling. Roll up, starting with long side. Seal seam. Place, seam side down, on greased baking sheet. Curve into crescent shape. Make slashes 1 inch apart just through top. Beat reserved egg white lightly; brush over dough. Sprinkle with mixture of 1 tablespoon sugar and cinnamon. Bake at 425° for 15 to 20 minutes. Makes 12 servings.

Coconut-Jam Coffee Cake

Make-ahead Quick Bread Mix makes this one fast—

  2 cups Quick Bread Mix
    (see page 7)
  ½ cup flaked coconut
  3 tablespoons sugar
  ½ teaspoon ground cinnamon
  1 beaten egg
  ½ cup milk
  ½ cup apricot-pineapple preserves
  1 tablespoon lemon juice

In bowl stir together Quick Bread Mix, coconut, sugar, and cinnamon. Add egg; mix well. Reserve ½ cup. To remaining mixture stir in milk. Spread in greased 8x8x2-inch baking pan. Combine preserves and lemon juice; spread over dough. Sprinkle with ½ cup reserved flour mixture. Bake at 350° for 35 to 40 minutes. Cool in pan; cut in squares. Serves 9.

Apple Dandy Rolls

Hot roll mix fix-ups shown on pages 8 and 9—

  1 13¾-ounce package hot roll mix
  ¾ cup warm water (110°)
  ¼ cup sugar
  ½ teaspoon ground nutmeg
  1 beaten egg
    Cranberry-Apple Filling

In bowl soften yeast from hot roll mix in water. Stir in sugar, nutmeg, egg, and hot roll mix; mix well. Cover and chill thoroughly, at least 2 hours. Roll dough to 18x10-inch rectangle on lightly floured surface. Cut in eighteen 10-inch strips. Roll each strip into a rope; coil strips loosely to form round rolls. Place on greased baking sheet. Make a slight indentation in center of each roll and fill with about 1 tablespoon Cranberry-Apple Filling. Let rise in warm place till about double (30 to 45 minutes). Bake at 375° about 15 minutes. While warm, drizzle with Confectioners' Icing (see recipe, page 13), if desired. Makes 18 rolls.

Cranberry-Apple Filling: In small saucepan combine 1 medium apple, peeled, cored, and chopped (1 cup); ½ cup fresh cranberries; and ½ cup sugar. Cook and stir over medium heat till apple is tender, 6 to 7 minutes. Remove from heat; stir in ¼ cup chopped walnuts and 1 tablespoon butter *or* margarine. Cool.

Iced Pecan Rolls

      1 cup all-purpose flour
      2 tablespoons granulated sugar
   1½ teaspoons baking powder
      ¼ teaspoon salt
      3 tablespoons butter *or* margarine
      ⅓ cup milk
      ½ cup ground pecans (2 ounces)
      ¼ cup sifted powdered sugar
      4 teaspoons water
      ½ teaspoon grated orange peel
      ¼ teaspoon vanilla
         Orange Confectioners' Icing

In mixing bowl stir together flour, granulated sugar, baking powder, and salt. Cut in butter till mixture resembles coarse crumbs. Stir in milk till mixture clings together. Knead gently on lightly floured surface (8 to 10 strokes). Roll or pat dough to 9x8-inch rectangle.

In bowl combine pecans and powdered sugar. Stir in water, orange peel, and vanilla. Spread pecan mixture over rectangle to within ½ inch of edges. Roll up, starting with long side. Seal seam well. Cut into nine 1-inch slices. Place, cut side down, in greased 8x1½-inch round baking pan. Bake at 375° for 25 to 30 minutes. Remove from pan. Drizzle with icing while warm. Makes 9 rolls.

Orange Confectioners' Icing: Mix ½ cup powdered sugar and 1 tablespoon orange juice.

Apple Butter Pull-Aparts

In mixing bowl stir together 2 cups all-purpose flour, 4 teaspoons baking powder, 1 tablespoon sugar, and ½ teaspoon salt. Cut in ½ cup shortening till mixture resembles coarse crumbs. Add ⅔ cup milk, stirring just till moistened. Knead on lightly floured surface (8 to 10 strokes). Roll dough to 16x8-inch rectangle.

Spread with 1 tablespoon softened butter. Combine ½ cup apple butter and ½ cup raisins; spread evenly over dough. Roll up, starting with long side. Seal seam well. Cut into sixteen 1-inch slices. Place, cut side down, in greased 8x8x2-inch baking pan. Spread surface of rolls with ¼ cup apple butter. Combine ¼ cup sugar and ¼ teaspoon ground cinnamon; sprinkle over top. Bake at 375° for 35 to 40 minutes. Remove from pan. Serve warm.

Caramel Rolls

      6 tablespoons butter *or* margarine
      ¾ cup caramel topping
      2 tablespoons milk
      ⅓ cup chopped pecans
      2 cups all-purpose flour
      ¼ cup sugar
      4 teaspoons baking powder
      1 beaten egg
      ½ cup milk
      ¼ cup cooking oil
      2 tablespoons sugar
      ¼ teaspoon ground cinnamon

Melt butter in 9x9x2-inch baking pan. Blend in topping and 2 tablespoons milk; spread evenly in bottom of pan. Sprinkle pecans in pan. In mixing bowl stir together flour, ¼ cup sugar, baking powder, and 1 teaspoon salt. Combine egg, ½ cup milk, and oil. Add to dry ingredients, stirring till dough clings together. Knead gently on lightly floured surface (8 to 10 strokes). Roll or pat dough to 12x10-inch rectangle. Combine remaining sugar and cinnamon; sprinkle over dough. Roll up, starting with long side. Cut into twelve 1-inch slices. Place, cut side down, in prepared pan. Bake at 400° for 20 to 25 minutes. Loosen sides and invert on serving plate; drizzle any remaining topping over rolls. Serve warm. Makes 12 rolls.

Quicky Sticky Rolls

Prepare 1 13¾-ounce package hot roll mix according to package directions and let rise. In saucepan melt ¼ cup butter; add 1 cup packed brown sugar and ¼ cup light corn syrup. Heat and stir till blended; do not boil. Pour into two 8½x4½x2½-inch loaf pans. Sprinkle ⅓ cup pecan halves in *each* pan. Roll dough to 20x12-inch rectangle on lightly floured surface. Spread with 2 tablespoons butter. Sprinkle with mixture of ½ cup granulated sugar and 1½ teaspoons ground cinnamon. Roll up, starting with long side. Seal seam well. Cut in twenty 1-inch slices. Place, cut side down, in pans. Let rise in warm place till nearly double (about 40 minutes). Bake at 375° about 25 minutes. Cool in pans 5 minutes. Loosen sides; invert on plate; drizzle any remaining topping over rolls. Makes 20 rolls.

Distinctive Loaves

Orange Nut Bread

2 cups all-purpose flour
¾ cup sugar
½ teaspoon salt
½ teaspoon baking soda
1 beaten egg
1 tablespoon grated orange peel
¾ cup orange juice
¼ teaspoon grated lemon peel
2 tablespoons lemon juice
2 tablespoons cooking oil
½ cup coarsely chopped walnuts

In mixing bowl stir together flour, sugar, salt, and soda. Combine egg, orange peel, orange juice, lemon peel, lemon juice, and oil. Add to dry ingredients, stirring just till moistened. Fold in nuts. Turn into greased 8½x4½x2½-inch loaf pan. Bake at 350° till done, 50 to 60 minutes. Cool in pan 10 minutes; remove from pan. Cool thoroughly. Wrap in foil; store overnight before slicing.

Prune Nut Bread

2¼ cups all-purpose flour
¾ cup sugar
½ cup wheat germ
1 tablespoon baking powder
¾ teaspoon salt
½ teaspoon ground cinnamon
1 beaten egg
1¼ cups milk
¼ cup cooking oil
1 cup drained cooked prunes,
    pitted and finely chopped
½ cup chopped nuts

In bowl thoroughly stir together the flour, sugar, wheat germ, baking powder, salt, and cinnamon. Combine egg, milk, and oil. Add to dry ingredients, stirring just till moistened. Fold in prunes and nuts. Turn into greased 9x5x3-inch loaf pan. Bake at 350° for 60 to 65 minutes. Cool in pan for 10 minutes; remove from pan. Cool thoroughly. Wrap in foil and store overnight before slicing.

Cherry-Pecan Bread

½ cup butter *or* margarine
¾ cup sugar
2 eggs
1 teaspoon vanilla
2 cups all-purpose flour
1 teaspoon baking soda
1 cup buttermilk
1 cup chopped pecans
1 10-ounce jar maraschino cherries,
    drained and chopped (1 cup)

Cream butter and sugar till light. Beat in eggs and vanilla. Stir together flour, soda, and ½ teaspoon salt; add alternately with buttermilk to creamed mixture, mixing well. Fold in nuts and cherries. Turn into greased 9x5x3-inch loaf pan. Bake at 350° for 55 to 60 minutes. Cool in pan 10 minutes; remove from pan. Cool. If desired, glaze with Confectioners' Icing (see recipe, page 13).

Quick Banana Bread

1 8-ounce package cream cheese,
    softened
1 cup sugar
1 cup mashed ripe banana
2 eggs
2 cups packaged biscuit mix *or*
    Quick Bread Mix (see page 7)
½ cup chopped pecans

Cream together cheese and sugar till light; beat in banana and eggs. Stir in biscuit mix and nuts just till moistened. Turn into greased 9x5x3-inch loaf pan. Bake at 350° for 60 to 65 minutes. Cover with foil last 15 minutes if bread browns too quickly. Cool in pan 10 minutes; remove from pan. Cool thoroughly.

Pour steaming coffee and icy cold milk to accompany refreshing slices of *Orange Nut Bread.* Tangy orange and lemon flavors mingle to make it the perfect breakfast bread. Serve it sliced with plenty of butter.

Orange-Date Nut Bread

    1 orange
    2¼ cups all-purpose flour
    ¾ cup sugar
    1 tablespoon baking powder
    ¾ teaspoon salt
    3 beaten eggs
    1 cup milk
    3 tablespoons butter *or* margarine,
       melted
    1 cup chopped pitted dates
    ¾ cup chopped walnuts

Quarter orange; remove peel. (Reserve meat of the orange for a salad.) Scrape white membrane from inside of peel; cut peel in thin strips and chop to make ⅔ cup. Cook peel in boiling water till tender; drain and dry.

In bowl stir together flour, sugar, baking powder, and salt. Combine eggs, milk, and butter. Add to dry ingredients, stirring just till moistened. Fold in peel, dates, and nuts. Turn into greased 9x5x3-inch loaf pan. Bake at 350° for 50 to 60 minutes. Cool in pan 10 minutes; remove from pan. Cool.

Devil's Food Tea Bread

Since the baked loaf doesn't fill the pan to the top, it makes perfect-sized slices for dainty tea sandwiches. Use softened cream cheese for the filling —

    3 cups all-purpose flour
    1 cup sugar
    ½ cup unsweetened cocoa powder
    1½ teaspoons baking soda
    1 beaten egg
    1¾ cups buttermilk
    ⅓ cup cooking oil
    1 teaspoon vanilla
    ¼ teaspoon red food coloring
       (optional)
    ½ cup chopped almonds

Thoroughly stir together flour, sugar, cocoa powder, soda, and 1 teaspoon salt. Combine egg, buttermilk, oil, vanilla, and food coloring. Add to dry ingredients, stirring just till moistened. Fold in nuts. Grease and flour bottoms only of two 8½x4½x2½-inch loaf pans. Turn batter into pans. Bake at 350° about 45 minutes. Cool in pans for 10 minutes; remove from pans. Cool. Wrap; store overnight.

Gumdrop Bread

Festive nut loaf shown on pages 8 and 9 —

    3 cups all-purpose flour
    ¾ cup sugar
    3½ teaspoons baking powder
    1 beaten egg
    1½ cups milk
    2 tablespoons cooking oil
    ¾ cup snipped gumdrops
    ½ cup chopped walnuts

In mixing bowl stir together flour, sugar, baking powder, and 1 teaspoon salt. Combine egg, milk, and oil. Add to dry ingredients, stirring just till moistened. Fold in gumdrops and nuts. Turn into greased and floured 9x5x3-inch loaf pan. Bake at 350° about 1 hour. Remove from pan immediately; cool thoroughly.

Cream Cheese-Filled Prune Bread

    1 teaspoon grated orange peel
    1 cup orange juice
    1 cup pitted dried prunes, snipped
       (6 ounces)
    2 3-ounce packages cream cheese,
       softened
    ⅓ cup sugar
    1 tablespoon all-purpose flour
    1 egg
    2 cups all-purpose flour
    ¾ cup sugar
    2 teaspoons baking powder
    ½ teaspoon baking soda
    2 beaten eggs
    2 tablespoons cooking oil
    ½ cup chopped walnuts

Combine orange peel, juice, and prunes; let stand 30 minutes. Combine cream cheese, ⅓ cup sugar, and 1 tablespoon flour; beat in 1 egg. Set aside. In bowl stir together 2 cups flour, ¾ cup sugar, baking powder, soda, and ½ teaspoon salt. Combine eggs, oil, prune mixture, and nuts. Add to dry ingredients, stirring just till moistened. Turn *half* the prune batter into greased and floured 9x5x3-inch loaf pan. Pour cream cheese mixture over. Spoon on remaining batter. Bake at 350° for 30 minutes; cover with foil and bake about 20 minutes more. Cool in pan 10 minutes; remove loaf. Cool. Wrap in foil; refrigerate overnight.

Banana Nut Bread

⅓ cup shortening
½ cup sugar
2 eggs
1¾ cups all-purpose flour
1 teaspoon baking powder
½ teaspoon baking soda
½ teaspoon salt
• • •
2 ripe medium bananas, mashed
(1 cup)
½ cup chopped walnuts

In mixing bowl cream shortening and sugar together well; beat in eggs. Thoroughly stir together the flour, baking powder, baking soda, and salt; add to creamed mixture alternately with banana, blending well after each addition. Fold in the nuts. Turn into greased 9x5x3-inch loaf pan. Bake at 350° till done, 45 to 50 minutes. Cool in pan on wire rack for 10 minutes; remove from pan. Cool thoroughly. Wrap and store overnight before slicing.

Irish Whole Wheat Soda Bread

3 cups all-purpose flour
1 cup whole wheat flour
2 teaspoons baking powder
1½ teaspoons baking soda
1 teaspoon salt
½ cup butter *or* margarine
1½ cups raisins
1 tablespoon caraway seed
2 well-beaten eggs
1½ cups buttermilk

In mixing bowl stir together all-purpose flour, whole wheat flour, baking powder, soda, and salt. Cut in butter till mixture is crumbly; stir in raisins and caraway seed. Reserve *1 tablespoon* beaten egg. Combine buttermilk and remaining egg; add to dry ingredients, stirring just till moistened. Knead gently on lightly floured surface (10 to 12 strokes). Shape dough into a ball; place in well-greased 2-quart casserole. With sharp knife, cut a 4-inch cross, ¼ inch deep, across center of loaf. Brush with reserved 1 tablespoon egg. Bake at 350° till wooden pick inserted in center comes out clean, 70 to 80 minutes. Remove from casserole. Cool thoroughly. Slice very thin.

Spiced Apple Revel Loaf

Layers of spiced apple filling show through on this loaf of bread shown on page 14 —

1 14-ounce jar spiced apple
rings
¼ cup packed brown sugar
¼ teaspoon ground cinnamon
¼ teaspoon ground nutmeg
¼ teaspoon ground ginger
¼ cup butter *or* margarine
1 cup granulated sugar
2 eggs
1 teaspoon vanilla
2½ cups all-purpose flour
1 tablespoon baking powder
1 teaspoon salt
1 teaspoon ground cinnamon
¾ cup milk
½ cup chopped walnuts

Peel apple rings; mash with a fork. Add brown sugar and next 3 spices; set aside. In bowl cream butter and granulated sugar together well. Beat in eggs and vanilla. Thoroughly stir together the flour, baking powder, salt, and 1 teaspoon cinnamon. Add alternately to creamed mixture with milk. Fold in nuts.

Spread a *third* of the batter into greased and floured 9x5x3-inch loaf pan. Drop a *third* of the apple mixture by tablespoons onto batter. Repeat layers to make 3 layers of each, ending with apple mixture. Bake at 350° about 60 minutes. Cool in pan 10 minutes; remove from pan. Cool thoroughly before slicing.

Fruited-Nut Coffee Bread

Dissolve 1 tablespoon instant coffee crystals in 1 cup boiling water; pour over 1¼ cups snipped pitted dates (8 ounces) and set aside.

In mixing bowl stir together 2¼ cups all-purpose flour, ¾ cup packed brown sugar, 2 teaspoons baking powder, ½ teaspoon baking soda, and ½ teaspoon salt. Combine 1 beaten egg; 1 large apple, peeled, cored, and shredded (1 cup); ½ cup chopped Brazil nuts; 2 tablespoons butter *or* margarine, melted; and date mixture. Add to dry ingredients, stirring just till moistened. Turn into greased 9x5x3-inch loaf pan. Bake at 350° for 60 to 65 minutes. Cool in pan 10 minutes; remove loaf. Cool.

Molasses Brown Bread

    ¼ cup shortening
    ½ cup sugar
    2 eggs
    1 cup applesauce
    ¼ cup light molasses
 1¼ cups all-purpose flour
    1 cup whole wheat flour
    2 teaspoons baking powder
    1 teaspoon baking soda

In bowl cream shortening and sugar together well. Beat in eggs. Add applesauce and molasses; mix well. Stir together both flours, baking powder, soda, and ½ teaspoon salt; add to creamed mixture, mixing well. Bake at 350° in one well-greased 8½x4½x2½-inch loaf pan for 50 to 55 minutes *or* in two well-greased 7½x3½x2-inch loaf pans for 30 to 35 minutes. Cool in pan 10 minutes; remove loaf. Cool. Makes 1 large or 2 small loaves.

Use well-greased and floured vegetable cans for baking quick breads. Fill cans only ⅔ full. After baking and cooling for specified time, cut off bottom of can to remove bread easily.

Fig-Raisin Bread

    1 cup orange juice
    1 cup finely snipped dried figs
    ½ cup raisins
    1 beaten egg
    ¾ cup sugar
    ½ teaspoon vanilla
 1½ cups all-purpose flour
    1 teaspoon baking powder
    ¼ teaspoon baking soda
    ½ cup chopped pecans

In saucepan combine orange juice, figs, and raisins; bring to boil. Remove from heat; cool. Combine egg, sugar, and vanilla. Add fig mixture; mix well. Stir together flour, baking powder, soda, and ¼ teaspoon salt; add to fig mixture, stirring just till moistened. Fold in nuts. Fill two well-greased and floured 16-ounce vegetable cans ⅔ full. Bake at 350° for 40 to 45 minutes. Cool in cans 5 minutes; turn out loaves. Cool thoroughly.

Apricot Nut Bread

    1 12-ounce can apricot nectar
    ¾ cup snipped dried apricots
    ½ cup raisins
    2 cups all-purpose flour
    1 cup sugar
    1 tablespoon baking powder
    1 beaten egg
    ⅓ cup milk
    2 tablespoons cooking oil
    ½ cup chopped almonds

In saucepan combine *1 cup* of the apricot nectar, apricots, and raisins; bring to boil. Cool. In bowl stir together flour, sugar, baking powder, and ½ teaspoon salt. Combine egg, milk, oil, and remaining nectar. Add to dry ingredients, stirring just till smooth. Fold in raisin mixture and nuts. Turn into greased and floured 9x5x3-inch loaf pan. Bake at 350° for 60 minutes. Cool in pan 10 minutes; remove loaf. Cool. Wrap and store overnight before slicing.

Bake an old-fashioned flavor treat from this ▶ bread buffet—*Molasses Brown Bread* (top), *Apricot Nut Bread*, *Potato-Corn Triangles* (see recipe, page 78), and *Fig-Raisin Bread*.

Zucchini Nut Loaf

Unusually good bread with cake-like texture —

- 1 cup grated unpeeled zucchini
- 1 cup sugar
- 1 egg
- ½ cup cooking oil

• • •

- 1½ cups all-purpose flour
- 1 teaspoon ground cinnamon
- ½ teaspoon salt
- ½ teaspoon baking soda
- ½ teaspoon ground nutmeg
- ¼ teaspoon baking powder
- ¼ teaspoon grated lemon peel
- ½ cup chopped walnuts

In mixing bowl beat zucchini, sugar, and egg together. Add oil; mix well. Stir together flour, cinnamon, salt, soda, nutmeg, baking powder, and lemon peel. Stir into zucchini mixture. Fold in nuts. Pour into a greased 8½x4½x2½-inch loaf pan. Bake at 325° till done, 60 to 65 minutes. Cool in pan for 10 minutes; remove from pan. Cool loaf thoroughly. Wrap and store loaf overnight before slicing.

Whole Wheat-Molasses Bread

Be sure to wrap and store these miniature, molasses-flavored loaves overnight before slicing —

- ½ cup shortening
- 2 tablespoons sugar
- 2 eggs
- ¾ cup light molasses
- 1 cup all-purpose flour
- 1 cup whole wheat flour
- ¾ teaspoon salt
- ¾ teaspoon baking soda
- ½ teaspoon ground ginger
- ½ teaspoon ground cinnamon
- ¾ cup buttermilk
- ½ cup chopped nuts

Cream shortening and sugar till light. Beat in eggs and molasses. Stir together both flours, salt, soda, ginger, and cinnamon. Add alternately with buttermilk to creamed mixture, beating after each addition. Fold in nuts. Bake in three greased and lightly floured 6x3x2-inch loaf pans at 350° about 35 minutes. Cool in pans for 10 minutes; remove from pans. Cool thoroughly. Wrap and store overnight.

Whole Wheat-Sesame Loaves

- 1 13¾-ounce package hot roll mix
- 1 cup whole wheat flour
- 1⅔ cups milk
- 1 egg
- 2 tablespoons milk
- 2 teaspoons sesame seed, toasted

In bowl stir together the flour from hot roll mix, whole wheat flour, and ½ teaspoon salt. Prepare dough following directions on hot roll mix package *except* use the 1⅔ cups milk and egg in place of water. Turn into two greased 7½x3½x2-inch loaf pans. Cover; let rise in warm place till doubled (about 45 minutes). Brush with 2 tablespoons milk and sprinkle with sesame seed. Bake at 375° for 35 to 40 minutes. Remove from pan. Cool.

Whole Wheat Quick Bread

- 2 cups whole wheat flour
- 1 teaspoon baking powder
- 1 teaspoon baking soda
- 1 beaten egg
- 1¾ cups buttermilk
- ¼ cup honey
- ¼ cup butter *or* margarine, melted
- ½ cup chopped walnuts
- ½ cup raisins

In mixing bowl stir together the flour, baking powder, soda, and 1 teaspoon salt. Combine egg, buttermilk, honey, and butter; add to dry ingredients, stirring just till moistened. Fold in nuts and raisins. Turn into greased 8½x4½x2½-inch loaf pan. Bake at 375° about 50 minutes. Remove from pan; cool thoroughly.

Cheesy Piccadilly Bread

In mixing bowl combine 1 beaten egg; ⅔ cup milk; ½ cup shredded sharp American cheese (2 ounces); ⅓ cup chopped dill pickle; 1 tablespoon cooking oil; and 1 tablespoon snipped parsley. Mix well. Add mixture to 2 cups packaged biscuit mix and stir just till moistened. Turn into greased 8x8x2-inch baking pan. Sprinkle with 2 tablespoons grated Parmesan cheese. Bake at 400° about 25 minutes. Serve warm. Makes 6 to 8 servings.

Don't worry about the crack that may form atop a quick bread loaf as it bakes. It's typical on most types of quick bread loaves.

Sherried Date and Nut Loaf

1 cup snipped pitted dates
⅔ cup dry sherry
1 tablespoon grated orange peel
2 cups all-purpose flour
⅔ cup packed brown sugar
⅓ cup wheat germ
2 teaspoons baking powder
1 teaspoon ground nutmeg
1 teaspoon salt
¼ teaspoon baking soda
2 beaten eggs
⅓ cup milk
¼ cup cooking oil
¾ cup coarsely chopped walnuts

In small bowl combine dates, sherry, and orange peel; set aside. Stir together flour, sugar, wheat germ, baking powder, nutmeg, salt, and soda. Combine eggs, milk, oil, and date mixture. Add dry ingredients, stirring just till moistened. Fold in nuts. Turn into greased 8½x 4½x2½-inch loaf pan. Bake at 350° for 50 to 55 minutes. Cool in pan for 10 minutes; remove loaf. Cool thoroughly. Wrap and store overnight before slicing.

Granola-Prune Bread

Toast slices of this special bread for breakfast; see it on the front cover—

2¾ cups all-purpose flour
¾ cup sugar
4 teaspoons baking powder
1½ teaspoons salt
2 beaten eggs
1⅓ cups milk
¼ cup cooking oil
1½ cups granola cereal
1 cup snipped pitted dried prunes
(about 6 ounces)

In mixing bowl stir together the flour, sugar, baking powder, and salt. Combine eggs, milk, and oil; add to flour mixture, stirring just till moistened. Fold in granola cereal and snipped prunes. Turn into greased 9x5x3-inch loaf pan. Bake at 350° till done, 65 to 70 minutes. Cool in pan on wire rack for 10 minutes; remove loaf. Cool thoroughly.

Cranberry Nut Bread

Make one big loaf or two small loaves of this red cranberry-flecked loaf—

½ cup butter *or* margarine,
softened
¾ cup sugar
1 egg
1 teaspoon grated orange peel
2½ cups all-purpose flour
1 tablespoon baking powder
1 teaspoon salt
¾ cup chopped fresh *or* frozen
cranberries
⅔ cup orange juice
⅓ cup milk
⅓ cup chopped almonds

In mixing bowl cream butter and sugar till fluffy. Beat in egg and orange peel. Stir together flour, baking powder, and salt. Combine cranberries, orange juice, and milk. Add alternately with dry ingredients to creamed mixture, mixing after each addition. Fold in nuts. Bake at 350° in one greased 8½x4½x2½-inch loaf pan about 60 minutes *or* bake in two greased 7½x 3½x2-inch loaf pans for 45 to 50 minutes. Cool in pans for 10 minutes; remove from pans. Cool. Makes 1 large or 2 small loaves.

Pineapple-Oatmeal Bread

1½ cups all-purpose flour
1 cup quick-cooking rolled oats
¾ cup packed brown sugar
2 teaspoons baking powder
½ teaspoon salt
1 beaten egg
1 8-ounce can crushed pineapple
⅓ cup cooking oil
⅓ cup milk
½ teaspoon vanilla
¼ cup chopped pecans
2 tablespoons quick-cooking
   rolled oats

In bowl stir together flour, 1 cup oats, sugar, baking powder, and salt. Combine egg, undrained pineapple, oil, milk, and vanilla. Add to dry ingredients, stirring just till moistened. Fold in nuts. Grease an 8½x4½x2½-inch loaf pan; sprinkle with 2 tablespoons oats. Turn batter into prepared pan. Bake at 350° for 60 to 65 minutes. Cool in pan for 10 minutes; remove loaf. Cool thoroughly. Wrap and store overnight at room temperature before slicing.

Soup Can Saffron Bread

¼ teaspoon saffron, crushed
¾ cup milk
5 tablespoons butter *or* margarine
¾ cup sugar
2 eggs
2 cups all-purpose flour
2½ teaspoons baking powder
½ cup raisins *or* dried currants
¼ cup chopped almonds, toasted

Dissolve saffron in milk; set aside. Cream butter and sugar till light. Beat in eggs. Stir together the flour, baking powder, and ½ teaspoon salt. Add about *three-fourths* of dry ingredients alternately with saffron milk to creamed mixture, beating well after each addition with electric mixer. By hand, stir in remaining dry ingredients. Fold in raisins and nuts. Bake in four well-greased 10- to 11-ounce soup cans *or* four well-greased 4½x2½x1½-inch loaf pans at 375° about 30 minutes, *or* two well-greased 7½x3½x2-inch loaf pans at 350° about 40 minutes. Cool 10 minutes; remove from pans. Cool. Makes 4 small or 2 large loaves.

Calypso Java Bread

1 tablespoon instant coffee
   crystals
½ cup milk
3 cups packaged biscuit mix *or*
   Quick Bread Mix (see page 7)
¾ cup packed brown sugar
¼ cup all-purpose flour
1 beaten egg
1 cup mashed ripe banana
1 cup snipped pitted dates
½ cup chopped walnuts

Dissolve coffee crystals in milk; set aside. In bowl stir together biscuit mix, sugar, and flour. Combine egg, banana, and coffee mixture. Add to dry ingredients, stirring just till moistened. Fold in dates and nuts. Grease bottoms only of two 1-pound coffee cans. Divide batter between two cans. Bake at 350° about 50 minutes. *Or,* bake in one greased 9x5x3-inch loaf pan at 350° for 55 to 60 minutes. Cool in pans for 10 minutes; remove from pans. Cool thoroughly. Makes 1 large or 2 small loaves.

Quick Poppy Seed-Lemon Loaf

3½ cups all-purpose flour
4 teaspoons baking powder
1 tablespoon poppy seed
1½ teaspoons salt
1 teaspoon grated lemon peel
3 beaten eggs
1¼ cups milk
¼ cup cooking oil
3 tablespoons honey

In bowl stir together flour, baking powder, poppy seed, salt, and lemon peel. Combine eggs, milk, oil, and honey. Add to dry ingredients, stirring just till moistened. Turn into two greased 7½x3½x2-inch loaf pans. Bake at 350° for 40 to 45 minutes. Cool in pans on rack for 10 minutes; remove from pans. Cut in slices and serve warm.

Treat the family to thin slices of easy-to-make ▶ *Calypso Java Bread* with whipped cream cheese and sweet marmalade for fun eating. Instant coffee crystals, banana, dates, and walnuts combine to flavor these round loaves.

Magical Muffins

Anytime is muffin time and you'll be even more convinced of this after you've tried just one of the many muffin varieties from this section. Best served piping hot from the oven, muffins have the versatile characteristic of having two personalities—sweet and spicy for dessert, or hearty and complementary to any kind of meal. Each type is a special treat in its own right.

For perfect muffins every time, follow the step-by-step picture guide at the beginning of the section. In addition, the basic muffin recipe and several variations are available for ready reference on the following pages.

Flip through the remaining pages, and you're sure to find many muffin ideas that you'll want to add to your quick bread repertoire.

Pop out a batch of fresh, moist muffins for nutritious nibbling. Try *Carrot-Pineapple Muffins, Half and Half Muffins, or Apple Butter Muffins* along with a cold dish of ice cream for dessert. (See Index for page numbers.)

Muffin Basics

Warm, tender muffins fresh from the oven are perfect meal partners regardless of the time of day they're served. Bake up a batch of fruit-flavored muffins for a breakfast, brunch, or coffee-time treat, serve bran muffins at lunch or dinner with butter and jam, or prepare corn muffins for supper as a base for main dish sauces, such as creamed turkey or beef. The uses for muffins are as limitless as the occasions you can imagine. Once you've tried the muffins in this section, your family is sure to ask for repeats of their favorites.

Because muffins are prepared with various types of flours, most of which are enriched, they contribute to a well-balanced diet. In addition to their importance in the regular diet, muffins are one quick bread that can be modified by people watching their dietary fat intake. For example, the specially tested low-fat recipe on the opposite page is made with less oil than the basic muffin recipe and it specifies skim milk. Also, substitute one egg white for the whole egg for those who are counting egg yolks in their diet.

Besides being a part of a good diet, muffins are quick and easy to prepare, once you understand some of the basic preparation pointers, storage techniques, and how to reheat muffins properly for serving.

The secret to good muffins is simple—proper mixing. Most muffins are prepared by first stirring all the dry ingredients together in a bowl, forming a well in the center of the dry ingredients, and adding the liquid ingredients all at once. Although sifting isn't necessary, the first mixing of the dry ingredients is important to ensure that the leavening is evenly distributed throughout the batter. The liquid ingredients—including the beaten egg, milk, or other liquid, and oil or melted fat are also combined before adding to the dry ingredients.

The most important step to remember is to stir the muffin batter just till the mixture is moistened. The batter will appear lumpy, not smooth. If overmixed, the muffins will have undesirable characteristics—they will be tough, have a peaked top, and they will have tunnels.

What you're looking for in the perfect muffin is a uniformly shaped muffin with a rounded top that's free from peaks. The crust is golden brown, tender, shiny, and pebbled or slightly rough. The insides of the basic muffins are creamy white or slightly yellow. And, it's large in proportion to its weight.

Sometimes you'll want to prepare muffins with a solid shortening, rather than oil or melted shortening. The method of mixing is slightly different to incorporate the fat. After the dry ingredients are stirred together thoroughly, the solid shortening is cut into the dry mixture until it's like coarse crumbs. At this point, the egg and milk mixture is added and the ingredients are stirred just till moistened.

Regardless of the mixing method, the final step in muffin preparation includes carefully spooning the batter into greased or paper bake cup-lined 2½-inch muffin pans (unless another size is specified in the recipe), filling the pans only ⅔ full. Avoid further mixing when spooning the batter into the pans. You can vary the size of the muffins to suit the occasion. For example, use miniature 1¾-inch muffin pans to bake dainty tea-sized muffins.

Finally, bake the muffins at the time and temperature specified in the recipe. Besides being overly browned, muffins baked too long will be dry and tough. On the other hand, underbaking results in pale, moist, heavy muffins.

Although muffins are at their best served warm from the oven, sometimes it becomes necessary to bake them up ahead of time. See photo at lower right for keeping muffins warm while the rest of the meal cooks. However, if necessary to store muffins longer, wrap cooled muffins in moisture-vaporproof material and freeze up to 2 months. Thaw in package at room temperature 1 hour or in a 250° to 300° oven till warmed throughout.

To reheat leftover muffins that haven't been frozen, sprinkle them lightly with water and wrap in foil or place in a brown paper bag. Heat the muffins at 400° for 15 to 20 minutes. Or, reheat muffins in a microwave oven on a paper napkin just till warm.

Best-Ever Muffins

See the popular sweet version of this muffin plus variations on page 34—

variations on page 34—

- 1¾ cups all-purpose flour*
- ¼ cup sugar
- 2½ teaspoons baking powder*
- ¾ teaspoon salt*
- 1 beaten egg
- ¾ cup milk
- ⅓ cup cooking oil *or* melted shortening

Stir together flour, sugar, baking powder, and salt; make a well in center. Combine egg, milk, and oil; add all at once to dry ingredients, stirring just till moistened. Fill greased *or* paper bake cup-lined muffin pans ⅔ full. Bake at 400° for 20 to 25 minutes. Makes 8 to 10.

Note: When substituting self-rising all-purpose flour, omit the baking powder and salt.

Enriched Best-Ever Muffins: Prepare Best-Ever Muffins as above *except* stir ⅓ cup nonfat dry milk powder in with dry ingredients.

Low-Fat Best-Ever Muffins: Prepare Best-Ever Muffins as above *except* substitute skim milk for whole milk and reduce cooking oil to 1 tablespoon. If desired, substitute 1 egg white for the whole egg.

Nutty Muffins: Prepare Best-Ever Muffins as above *except* stir ½ cup chopped peanuts *or* macadamia nuts into dry ingredients.

Shown top right: The muffin batter should appear lumpy; do not attempt to stir till a smooth batter results. **Middle:** Push the muffin batter from spoon with rubber spatula into prepared muffin pans, filling pans only ⅔ full. This allows space for rising and yields perfect size muffins. For many muffins you can line the pans with paper bake cups to make cleanup a little easier. **Bottom:** When muffins are ready before the rest of the meal is completed, tip them to one side in muffin pan to keep them from steaming and becoming soggy. Serve warm muffins with butter or your favorite spread, if desired. Store any leftover muffins in a covered container or wrap in moisture-vaporproof material and freeze.

Sugar-and-Spice Muffins

Sweet Best-Ever Muffins

Use this basic recipe to create your own wonderful, sweet muffin recipes. Toss in some fruit, alter the liquid, or dress up the tops —

>   1¾ cups all-purpose flour
>   ½ cup sugar
>   2½ teaspoons baking powder
>   ¾ teaspoon salt
>   1 beaten egg
>   ¾ cup milk
>   ⅓ cup cooking oil *or* melted
>   shortening

Stir together flour, sugar, baking powder, and salt; make a well in center. Combine egg, milk, and oil; add all at once to dry ingredients, stirring just till moistened. Fill greased *or* paper bake cup-lined muffin pans ⅔ full. Bake at 375° for 18 to 20 minutes. Makes 8 to 10.

Pineapple-Pecan Muffins: Prepare Sweet Best-Ever Muffins as above *except* drain one 8-ounce can crushed pineapple (juice pack), reserving the juice; add enough milk to juice to equal ¾ cup. Combine the juice-milk mixture with egg, oil, and crushed pineapple. Stir this mixture into the dry ingredients just till moistened. Fill prepared muffin pans ⅔ full. Sprinkle ⅓ cup chopped pecans over tops. Bake as above. Makes 10 to 12.

Chocolate Chip Muffins: Prepare Sweet Best-Ever Muffins as above *except* add enough milk to juice of one orange to make ¾ cup. Combine orange-milk mixture with egg, oil, and 2 teaspoons grated orange peel. Mix as directed, then carefully fold ½ cup semisweet chocolate pieces into muffin batter. Makes 10 to 12.

Cinnamon-Apple-Raisin Muffins: Prepare Sweet Best-Ever Muffins as above *except* stir ½ teaspoon ground cinnamon in with dry ingredients. Mix as directed, then carefully fold 1 cup chopped, peeled apple and ⅓ cup raisins into batter. Bake for 20 to 25 minutes. While warm, dip tops in melted butter *or* margarine, then in sugar. Makes 12 muffins.

Rhubarb-Orange Muffins

>   2 cups finely diced rhubarb
>   ¾ cup sugar
>   1 teaspoon grated orange peel
>   2½ cups all-purpose flour
>   1½ teaspoons baking powder
>   1 teaspoon baking soda
>   ½ teaspoon salt
>   2 beaten eggs
>   ¾ cup buttermilk
>   3 tablespoons butter *or* margarine,
>   melted
>   Sifted powdered sugar

Combine rhubarb, ¼ *cup* of the sugar, and orange peel; let stand 5 minutes. Stir together flour, ½ cup sugar, baking powder, baking soda, and salt. Combine eggs, buttermilk, and butter; add all at once to dry ingredients, stirring just till moistened. Gently fold in rhubarb mixture. Fill greased muffin pans ⅔ full. Bake at 375° for 20 to 25 minutes. Dust warm muffins with powdered sugar. Makes 16 muffins.

Cranberry-Orange Rumbas

These little beauties are shown on page 66 —

>   1 egg
>   1 cup cranberry-orange relish
>   ⅓ cup milk
>   ¼ teaspoon rum flavoring
>   1 14-ounce package apple-cinnamon
>   muffin mix

In medium mixing bowl beat egg; stir in cranberry-orange relish, milk, and rum flavoring. Add muffin mix, stirring with fork just till moistened. Fill greased *or* paper bake cup-lined muffin pans ⅔ full. Bake at 400° till done, 20 to 25 minutes. Makes 12 muffins.

Fresh, diced rhubarb and tangy grated orange peel give the mouth-watering flavor to *Rhubarb-Orange Muffins.* Dust the warm muffin tops with sweet powdered sugar just before serving them to the muffin lovers in your family.

Orange-Cinnamon Muffins

Sugar and spice topper makes this one tasty—

1 cup all-purpose flour
¼ cup sugar
1 tablespoon baking powder
½ teaspoon salt
1 cup quick-cooking rolled oats
1 beaten egg
1 teaspoon grated orange peel
½ cup orange juice
¼ cup milk
3 tablespoons cooking oil
2 tablespoons sugar
1 tablespoon all-purpose flour
1 teaspoon butter *or* margarine,
    melted
¼ teaspoon ground cinnamon

Stir together 1 cup flour, ¼ cup sugar, baking powder, and salt. Stir in oats. Combine egg, orange peel, orange juice, milk, and oil; add all at once to dry ingredients, stirring just till moistened. Fill greased muffin pans ⅔ full. Thoroughly combine the remaining ingredients and sprinkle over batter in muffin pans. Bake at 425° till golden brown, about 15 minutes. Makes 12 muffins.

Apple Butter Muffins

A quick-to-make muffin shown on pages 30 and 31—

1 beaten egg
½ cup milk
2 tablespoons sugar
2 tablespoons cooking oil
• • •
2 cups packaged biscuit mix
½ cup chopped walnuts
¼ cup apple butter
    Spicy Topping

In mixing bowl combine egg, milk, sugar, and oil. Add biscuit mix; beat vigorously 30 seconds. Fold in chopped walnuts. Fill paper bake cup-lined muffin pans ⅓ full. Top each with *1 teaspoon* apple butter. Cover with remaining batter till ⅔ full. Sprinkle with Spicy Topping. Bake at 400° for 20 to 25 minutes. Makes 12.

Spicy Topping: Combine 2 tablespoons packed brown sugar, 1 tablespoon all-purpose flour, and ¼ teaspoon ground cinnamon. Cut in 2 teaspoons butter *or* margarine till crumbly.

Orange Breakfast Muffins

2 cups all-purpose flour
⅓ cup sugar
1 teaspoon baking powder
¾ teaspoon salt
½ teaspoon baking soda
2 beaten eggs
1 tablespoon grated orange peel
1 cup orange juice
⅓ cup cooking oil
¼ cup orange marmalade

Thoroughly stir together the flour, sugar, baking powder, salt, and baking soda. Combine eggs, orange peel, orange juice, and oil; add all at once to dry ingredients, stirring just till moistened. Fill greased muffin pans ⅔ full. Bake at 400° for 20 to 25 minutes. Heat orange marmalade till melted; brush over tops of hot muffins. Makes 12 muffins.

Easy Apple Fantans

1¾ cups all-purpose flour
¼ cup sugar
2½ teaspoons baking powder
¾ teaspoon salt
½ teaspoon ground cinnamon
1 beaten egg
¾ cup milk
⅓ cup cooking oil
½ cup finely chopped, peeled
    tart apple
• • •
3 tablespoons sugar
½ teaspoon ground cinnamon
    Dash ground nutmeg
1 tart apple, peeled and thinly sliced

Stir together flour, ¼ cup sugar, baking powder, salt, and ½ teaspoon ground cinnamon; make well in center. Combine egg, milk, and oil; add all at once to dry ingredients, stirring just till moistened. Fold in finely chopped apple. Fill greased muffin pans ⅔ full.

In small bowl combine 3 tablespoons sugar, ½ teaspoon ground cinnamon, and nutmeg; coat apple slices with spice mixture. Press 2 or 3 apple slices into top of each muffin to make stripes. Bake at 400° for 20 to 25 minutes. If desired, brush tops of hot muffins with melted butter. Makes 10 to 12 muffins.

Sunshine Muffins

These fresh-tasting pineapple- and orange-flavored muffins are great for breakfast—

    1 8¼-ounce can crushed pineapple
      Milk
    1½ cups Quick Bread Mix
       (see page 7)
    3 tablespoons sugar
    1 beaten egg
    1 tablespoon sugar
    1 tablespoon grated orange peel

Drain pineapple, reserving syrup. Add milk to reserved syrup to make ¾ cup. In bowl combine Quick Bread Mix and 3 tablespoons sugar. Combine egg, syrup mixture, and ¼ *cup* of the drained pineapple; add all at once to dry ingredients, stirring just till moistened. Fill greased *or* paper bake cup-lined muffin pans ⅔ full. Stir together remaining drained pineapple, 1 tablespoon sugar, and grated orange peel. Spoon about *1 tablespoon* pineapple mixture atop batter in each muffin pan. Bake at 400° for 20 to 25 minutes. Makes 8 muffins.

Orange-Date Muffins

    1¾ cups all-purpose flour
     2 tablespoons sugar
    2½ teaspoons baking powder
     ¾ teaspoon salt
     1 beaten egg
     1 tablespoon finely grated orange
        peel (set aside)
     ¾ cup orange juice
     ⅓ cup cooking oil *or* melted
        shortening
     ⅔ cup chopped pitted dates
     2 tablespoons melted butter *or*
        margarine
     3 tablespoons sugar

Thoroughly stir together the flour, 2 tablespoons sugar, baking powder, and salt. Combine egg, orange juice, and cooking oil; add all at once to dry ingredients, stirring just till moistened. Fold in dates. Fill greased muffin pans *or* paper bake cup-lined muffin pans ⅔ full. Bake at 400° for 20 to 25 minutes. Dip tops in melted butter and then in a mixture of 3 tablespoons sugar and the grated orange peel. Makes 10 to 12 muffins.

Cranberry-Nut Muffins

Pretty red cranberry flecks add tartness to this spicy, moist muffin—

    1 cup fresh cranberries, coarsely
       chopped
    ¼ cup sugar
    1¾ cups all-purpose flour
    ¼ cup sugar
    1 tablespoon baking powder
    1 teaspoon salt
    ½ teaspoon ground cinnamon
    ¼ teaspoon ground allspice
             • • •
    1 beaten egg
    ¼ teaspoon grated orange peel
    ¾ cup orange juice
    ⅓ cup butter *or* margarine, melted
    ¼ cup chopped walnuts

Toss cranberries with ¼ cup sugar; set aside. Thoroughly stir together the flour, ¼ cup sugar, baking powder, salt, and spices; make well in center. Combine egg, orange peel, orange juice, and melted butter; add all at once to dry ingredients, stirring just till moistened. Gently fold in cranberry mixture and nuts. Fill greased *or* paper bake cup-lined muffin pans ⅔ full. Bake at 400° for 20 to 25 minutes. Makes 12 muffins.

Dip tops of warm muffins in melted butter *or* margarine and then in granulated sugar for a sweet and sparkling, crusty topping.

Because they start with the easy Quick Bread Mix, cranberry-filled *Polka Dot Muffins* can be made in a jiffy. Another speedy recipe using the Quick Bread Mix is the *Berry-Topped Banana Waffles* (see recipe, page 73), topped with strawberries and ice cream-yogurt topping.

Polka Dot Muffins

Cranberry muffins made with Quick Bread Mix—

- 1 cup fresh cranberries, chopped
- ½ cup sugar
- 1 beaten egg
- ½ cup orange juice
- ¼ cup sugar
- 2 tablespoons cooking oil
- 2 cups Quick Bread Mix (see page 7)

Mix cranberries and the ½ cup sugar; set aside. Combine egg, orange juice, the ¼ cup sugar, and cooking oil; add all at once to Quick Bread Mix, stirring just till moistened. Fold in cranberry mixture. Fill greased *or* paper bake cup-lined muffin pans ⅔ full. Bake at 400° about 20 minutes. Makes 12 muffins.

Honey-Wheat Muffins

- 1 cup all-purpose flour
- ½ cup whole wheat flour
- 2 teaspoons baking powder
- ½ teaspoon salt
- 1 beaten egg
- ½ cup milk
- ½ cup honey
- ¼ cup cooking oil
- ½ teaspoon grated lemon peel

Thoroughly stir together both flours, baking powder, and salt; make a well in center. Combine egg, milk, honey, oil, and lemon peel; add all at once to dry ingredients, stirring just till moistened. Fill greased *or* paper bake cup-lined muffin pans ⅔ full. Bake at 400° for 18 to 22 minutes. Makes 10 muffins.

Carrot-Pineapple Muffins

A very tender muffin pictured on pages 30 and 31 —

> 1 8¼-ounce can crushed pineapple
> Milk
> 2 cups all-purpose flour
> ⅓ cup packed brown sugar
> 1 tablespoon baking powder
> ½ teaspoon salt
> 1 beaten egg
> ¾ cup finely shredded carrot
> ⅓ cup cooking oil
> ½ teaspoon vanilla
> 2 tablespoons granulated sugar
> ½ teaspoon ground cinnamon

Drain pineapple, reserving syrup; add milk to syrup to equal ¾ cup. Stir together the flour, brown sugar, baking powder, and salt. Combine egg, carrot, milk-syrup mixture, drained pineapple, oil, and vanilla; add all at once to dry ingredients, stirring just till moistened. Fill greased *or* paper bake cup-lined muffin pans ⅔ full. Sprinkle tops with a mixture of the remaining ingredients. Bake at 400° for 20 to 25 minutes. Makes 12 muffins.

Half and Half Muffins

Two-toned muffins shown on pages 30 and 31 —

> 2 cups all-purpose flour
> ¼ cup granulated sugar
> 1 tablespoon baking powder
> ¾ teaspoon salt
> ¼ cup sweetened cocoa mix
> ¼ cup chopped walnuts
> 1 beaten egg
> ¾ cup milk
> ¼ cup butter *or* margarine, melted
> 2 tablespoons dairy sour cream
> Sifted powdered sugar

Stir together the flour, granulated sugar, baking powder, and salt. Divide mixture between two bowls. Stir cocoa mix and nuts into one. Beat together egg, milk, butter, and sour cream. Add *half* the liquid ingredients to *each* portion of dry ingredients; stir each just till moistened. Spoon about 2 tablespoons cocoa mixture and 2 tablespoons plain mixture side by side in each well-greased muffin pan filling pans ⅔ full. Bake at 400° about 20 minutes. Dust with powdered sugar. Makes 10 to 12.

Lemon-Blueberry Muffins

Make these lemon-sparked muffins with plump, fresh blueberries when berries are in season —

> 1 beaten egg
> 2 cups packaged biscuit mix
> ⅓ cup sugar
> 2 tablespoons butter *or*
>   margarine, softened
> 1 lemon
>   Milk
> 1 cup fresh blueberries *or*
>   frozen whole blueberries,
>   thawed and drained
>   Melted butter *or* margarine
> 2 tablespoons sugar

In mixing bowl combine egg, biscuit mix, ⅓ cup sugar, and 2 tablespoons butter. Grate 1 tablespoon lemon peel; set aside. Squeeze lemon; add enough milk to lemon juice to make ⅔ cup liquid. Add to biscuit mixture; mix well. Fold in blueberries. Fill paper bake cup-lined muffin pans ⅔ full. Bake at 400° about 25 minutes. While warm, dip muffin tops in melted butter, then in a mixture of 2 tablespoons sugar and the grated lemon peel. Makes 12 muffins.

Brownie Muffins

Treat yourself and family to big glasses of icy milk and these brownie-tasting muffins —

> 1¾ cups all-purpose flour
> ½ cup sugar
> 3 tablespoons unsweetened cocoa
>   powder
> 2½ teaspoons baking powder
> ¾ teaspoon salt
> ½ teaspoon ground cinnamon
> 1 beaten egg
> ¾ cup milk
> ⅓ cup cooking oil *or* melted shortening
> ⅓ cup chopped nuts

Thoroughly stir together the flour, sugar, cocoa powder, baking powder, salt, and cinnamon; make a well in center. Combine egg, milk, and oil; add all at once to dry ingredients, stirring just till moistened. Fold in chopped nuts. Fill greased *or* paper bake cup-lined muffin pans ⅔ full. Bake at 400° for 18 to 20 minutes. Makes 12 muffins.

Perfect Meal-Mate Muffins

Bran Muffins

1½ cups whole bran cereal
1 cup buttermilk
1 cup all-purpose flour
2 teaspoons baking powder
½ teaspoon baking soda
½ teaspoon salt
⅓ cup packed brown sugar

• • •

1 beaten egg
¼ cup cooking oil *or* melted
  shortening
¾ cup raisins *or* snipped pitted
  dates (optional)

Combine bran and buttermilk; let stand till liquid is absorbed, about 3 minutes. In mixing bowl stir together flour, baking powder, baking soda, and salt, Stir in brown sugar. Combine cereal-milk mixture, egg, and oil or melted shortening; add all at once to dry ingredients, stirring just till moistened. (Batter will be thick.) Fold in raisins or dates, if desired. Fill greased muffin pans ⅔ full. Bake at 400° for 20 to 25 minutes. Makes 10 to 12 muffins.

Sunflower-Whole Wheat Muffins

This full-bodied muffin is seen on page 4 —

1½ cups whole wheat flour
½ cup all-purpose flour
2½ teaspoons baking powder
¾ teaspoon salt
½ cup shelled sunflower seed
1 beaten egg
¾ cup milk
⅓ cup cooking oil
⅓ cup honey

In bowl thoroughly stir together whole wheat flour, all-purpose flour, baking powder, and salt; stir in sunflower seed. Make well in center. Combine egg, milk, oil, and honey; add all at once to dry ingredients, stirring just till dry ingredients are moistened. Fill greased muffin pans ⅔ full. Bake at 400° for 20 to 25 minutes. Makes 12 muffins.

Carrot Muffins

Fresh carrot adds texture to these muffins —

1 cup all-purpose flour
¼ cup packed brown sugar
2 teaspoons baking powder
½ teaspoon salt
2 beaten eggs
1 cup finely shredded carrot
¼ cup cooking oil
1 tablespoon lemon juice

Thoroughly stir together flour, brown sugar, baking powder, and salt; make well in center. Combine eggs, carrot, oil, and lemon juice; add all at once to dry ingredients, stirring just till moistened. Fill well-greased *or* paper bake cup-lined muffin pans ⅔ full. Bake at 400° for 18 to 20 minutes. Makes 8 muffins.

Cereal Muffins

Taste these wheat-flavored muffins soon —

1 cup all-purpose flour
¼ cup sugar
2 teaspoons baking powder
½ teaspoon baking soda
½ teaspoon salt
⅓ cup shortening
2 cups whole wheat flakes
1 beaten egg
1 cup buttermilk

Thoroughly stir together the flour, sugar, baking powder, baking soda, and salt. Cut in shortening till mixture resembles coarse crumbs. Stir in wheat flakes. Combine egg and buttermilk; add all at once to dry ingredients, stirring just till moistened. Fill greased *or* paper bake cup-lined muffin pans ⅔ full. Bake at 400° for 18 to 20 minutes. Makes 8 or 9 muffins.

Include wholesome *Bran Muffins* as the perfect mealtime accompaniment to round out lunch, supper, or dinner. The delicious homemade bran-flavored muffins can be further enhanced by the addition of raisins or dates.

Salad Dressing Muffins

Made with cheese Italian salad dressing mix, these muffins go well with a hearty bowl of soup—

    2 cups all-purpose flour
    2 tablespoons sugar
    ½ envelope cheese Italian salad
        dressing mix (about 2
        tablespoons)
    1 tablespoon baking powder
    ¼ teaspoon salt
    1 beaten egg
    1 cup milk
    ¼ cup cooking oil *or* melted
        shortening

Thoroughly stir together the flour, sugar, salad dressing mix, baking powder, and salt. Combine egg, milk, and oil; add all at once to dry ingredients, stirring just till moistened. Fill greased muffin pans ⅔ full. Bake at 400° for 20 to 25 minutes. Makes 10 muffins.

Refrigerator Bran Muffins

Have a batch of these convenient muffins on hand in the refrigerator. Then, bake as needed—

    4 cups whole bran cereal
        (9 ounces)
    2 cups crushed shredded wheat biscuits
        (3 ounces)
    2 cups boiling water
    1 cup shortening
    4 cups buttermilk
    4 beaten eggs
        • • •
    5 cups all-purpose flour
    2 cups sugar
    1 tablespoon baking powder
    1 tablespoon baking soda
    2 teaspoons salt

In large bowl combine cereals; stir in boiling water. Stir in shortening until melted. Add buttermilk and eggs; mix well. Stir together flour, sugar, baking powder, baking soda, and salt. Add all at once to cereal mixture, stirring just till moistened. Store in tightly covered container in refrigerator up to 4 weeks. To bake, fill greased muffin pans ⅔ full. Bake at 400° for 23 to 28 minutes. (Note: Baking time will increase the longer the batter is stored.) Makes 13½ cups batter which yields 54 muffins.

Protein-Plus Muffins

    1¼ cups soy flour
    ⅔ cup nonfat dry milk powder
    2 teaspoons baking powder
    2 beaten eggs
    1 teaspoon grated orange peel
    ¾ cup orange juice
    2 tablespoons honey
    2 tablespoons cooking oil
    ½ cup chopped pitted dates
    ¼ cup chopped nuts

Stir together the soy flour, milk powder, baking powder, and ½ teaspoon salt. Combine next 5 ingredients; add to dry ingredients, stirring just till moistened. Fold in dates and nuts. Fill greased muffin pans ⅔ full. Bake at 350° about 30 minutes. Makes 12 muffins.

Onion Supper Muffins

    ¼ cup chopped onion
    1 tablespoon butter *or* margarine
    1 14-ounce package corn muffin mix
    ½ cup dairy sour cream
    ½ cup shredded sharp American
        cheese (2 ounces)

Cook onion in butter till tender. Prepare muffin mix according to package directions, adding the onion. Fill greased muffin pans ⅔ full. Mix sour cream and cheese; spoon about *1 teaspoon* atop batter in *each* pan. Bake at 400° for 15 to 20 minutes. Cool in pan 5 minutes before removing. Makes 10 to 12 muffins.

Whole Wheat Muffins

    ¼ cup shelled pumpkin seed
    1½ cups whole wheat flour
    ½ cup all-purpose flour
    2½ teaspoons baking powder
    1 beaten egg
    ¾ cup milk
    ⅓ cup cooking oil
    ⅓ cup light molasses

Chop pumpkin seed. Combine with next 3 ingredients and ¾ teaspoon salt. Combine remaining ingredients; add to dry mixture. Mix till moistened. Fill greased muffin pans ⅔ full. Bake at 400° for 20 to 25 minutes. Makes 12.

Two-Cheese Muffins

Good accompaniment for a fruit salad—

1½ **cups all-purpose flour**
½ **cup yellow cornmeal**
¼ **cup sugar**
1 **tablespoon baking powder**
¾ **teaspoon salt**
½ **cup shredded sharp Cheddar**
   cheese (2 ounces)
1 **beaten egg**
1 **cup milk**
½ **cup cream-style cottage cheese**
¼ **cup cooking oil** *or* **melted**
   shortening

Thoroughly stir together the flour, cornmeal, sugar, baking powder, and salt; stir in shredded cheese. Combine egg, milk, cottage cheese, and cooking oil; add all at once to dry ingredients, stirring just till moistened. Fill well-greased muffin pans ⅔ full. Bake at 400° for 20 to 25 minutes. Makes 12 muffins.

Peppy Pepper Muffins

This green-flecked muffin is seen on page 2—

1¼ **cups all-purpose flour**
½ **cup yellow cornmeal**
2 **tablespoons sugar**
2½ **teaspoons baking powder**
1 **teaspoon chili powder**
¾ **teaspoon salt**
1 **beaten egg**
¾ **cup milk**
⅓ **cup cooking oil**
2 **tablespoons finely chopped**
   green pepper
1 **tablespoon finely chopped onion**

Thoroughly stir together the flour, cornmeal, sugar, baking powder, chili powder, and salt. Combine egg, milk, cooking oil, green pepper, and onion; add all at once to dry ingredients, stirring just till moistened. Fill greased muffin pans ⅔ full. Bake at 400° for 20 to 25 minutes. Makes 8 muffins.

Set a big basket of *Two-Cheese Muffins* on the table to complement any luncheon or dinner menu. Serve them warm from the oven with lots of whipped butter. For a change, substitute Swiss cheese or a milder Cheddar for the sharp Cheddar cheese specified in the recipe.

Set a pat of butter atop warm *Sausage Supper Muffins* and you'll enjoy the muffin's hearty sausage and cheese goodness. Almost a meal in themselves, the muffins are the perfect accompaniment for a late evening supper served with eggs, fruit, and a piping hot beverage.

Sausage Supper Muffins

    8 ounces bulk pork sausage
    1 cup all-purpose flour
    1 cup yellow cornmeal
    ½ cup grated Parmesan cheese
    ¼ cup sugar
    4 teaspoons baking powder
    2 teaspoons snipped
      chives (optional)
    2 beaten eggs
    1 cup milk
    ¼ cup cooking oil

Brown sausage, stirring to break into small pieces; drain off fat. Stir together next 6 ingredients and ¾ teaspoon salt. Combine eggs, milk, and oil; add all at once to dry ingredients, stirring just till moistened. Fold in sausage. Fill greased muffin pans ⅔ full. Bake at 425° for 20 to 25 minutes. Makes 12 muffins.

Mexican Muffins

Zippy muffin shown on the cover—

    2 cups all-purpose flour
    2 tablespoons sugar
    1 tablespoon baking powder
    ⅛ teaspoon chili powder
    1 beaten egg
    1 8-ounce can cream-style corn
    ⅓ cup milk
    3 tablespoons cooking oil
    2 tablespoons chopped canned green
      chili peppers
    2 tablespoons chopped canned
      pimiento

Stir together first 4 ingredients and 1 teaspoon salt. Combine remaining ingredients; add all at once to dry ingredients, stirring just till moistened. Fill greased muffin pans ⅔ full. Bake at 400° for 20 to 25 minutes. Makes 12.

Flavortop Muffins

This dinner muffin is attractively topped with pimiento, parsley, and green onion—

1¾ cups all-purpose flour
2 tablespoons sugar
2½ teaspoons baking powder
¾ teaspoon salt
1 beaten egg
¾ cup buttermilk
⅓ cup cooking oil

• • •

1 3-ounce package cream cheese,
　softened
2 tablespoons butter *or* margarine,
　softened
1 tablespoon chopped canned
　pimiento
1 tablespoon snipped parsley
2 teaspoons finely chopped
　green onion

In mixing bowl thoroughly stir together the flour, sugar, baking powder, and salt; make a well in center. Combine egg, buttermilk, and cooking oil; add all at once to dry ingredients, stirring just till moistened. Fill greased muffin pans ⅔ full. Blend together remaining ingredients. Top batter in *each* muffin pan with about *1 tablespoon* cheese mixture. Bake at 400° for 20 to 25 minutes. Makes 10 muffins.

Rye Muffins

Caraway seed adds distinctive flavor—

1 cup all-purpose flour
1 cup rye flour
2 tablespoons packed brown sugar
4 teaspoons baking powder
1 teaspoon salt
¾ teaspoon caraway seed

• • •

1 beaten egg
1 cup milk
¼ cup cooking oil

In mixing bowl thoroughly stir together the all-purpose flour, rye flour, brown sugar, baking powder, salt, and caraway seed; make a well in center. Combine the egg, milk, and oil. Add all at once to dry ingredients, stirring just till moistened. Fill greased muffin pans ⅔ full. Bake at 400° for 15 to 18 minutes. Makes 10.

Bacon and Egg Muffins

Just the right muffin to serve for breakfast—

2 cups all-purpose flour
2 tablespoons sugar
4 teaspoons baking powder
1 teaspoon dry mustard
½ teaspoon salt
¾ cup shredded sharp American
　cheese (3 ounces)

• • •

1 beaten egg
¾ cup milk
¼ cup cooking oil

• • •

2 hard-cooked eggs, chopped
4 slices bacon, crisp-cooked,
　drained, and crumbled

In mixing bowl thoroughly stir together the flour, sugar, baking powder, dry mustard, and salt; stir in the shredded cheese. Make a well in center of dry ingredients. Combine egg, milk, and oil; add all at once to dry ingredients, stirring just till moistened. Fill well-greased muffin pans ⅓ full. Combine chopped egg and crumbled bacon; divide mixture evenly among muffin pans. Top with remaining batter filling muffin pans ⅔ full. Bake at 400° for 20 to 25 minutes. Makes 12 muffins.

Chip-Topped Cheese Muffins

1¾ cups all-purpose flour
1 tablespoon sugar
1 tablespoon baking powder
¾ teaspoon salt
1 cup shredded sharp American
　cheese (4 ounces)

• • •

1 beaten egg
¾ cup milk
¼ cup cooking oil
⅓ cup crushed potato chips

In mixing bowl thoroughly stir together the flour, sugar, baking powder, and salt; stir in the cheese. Make a well in center. Combine the egg, milk, and oil; add all at once to dry ingredients, stirring just till moistened. Fill well-greased muffin pans ⅔ full. Top with crushed potato chips. Bake at 375° for 20 to 25 minutes. Makes 12 muffins.

Praiseworthy Biscuits

Homemade biscuits taste great! When served with butter and drenched with golden honey, biscuits turn any meal into a special treat.

To get started on the right track, read the first two pages of this section for handy tips, which include a picture guide and the basic biscuit recipe. You'll want to refer here often.

Then, try some of the other popular biscuit recipes that follow. But don't stop there—go on to the section in which you twist, cut, fold, stack, or drop biscuit dough into interesting shapes. You're sure to develop some of your own creations after trying some of these recipe ideas.

One word of caution—be ready for compliments and refill requests when you bake up batches of the taste-tempting biscuits.

These attractive biscuits are more than just sidekicks to complete the meal. Try *Sweet Potato Biscuits, Whole Wheat Drop Biscuits, Pecan Petal Biscuits,* or *Bacon Biscuit Bars* and see for yourself. (See Index for page numbers.)

Biscuit Basics

Coast to coast, people enjoy biscuits hot from the oven and spread generously with butter. However, food preferences and ingredients in various sections of the country often determine what type of biscuit is typical. For example, the North enjoys tall, tender, flaky biscuits, whereas the South takes pride in its biscuits with a soft, tender crumb. The more tender crumb of the Southern-style biscuit is due to the soft wheat flour generally available in this area of the country. Soft wheat flour has a lower gluten content — gluten forms the framework that gives bread its structure.

People in a hurry often prepare drop biscuits because of their ease of preparation. This biscuit variation is made with standard ingredients; however more liquid is added for a drop biscuit. The thick batter is dropped from a spoon, rather than rolled and cut with a biscuit cutter like the usual baking powder biscuits.

You'll find that standard biscuits are not much more difficult to make than the drop variety, once the techniques for preparing biscuits are mastered. In fact, mixing up and baking a batch of baking powder biscuits is relatively simple.

Since there is no need to sift the dry ingredients, the first step is to stir the flour, baking powder, and salt together well to evenly distribute the leavening and salt.

Next, cut the shortening into the dry ingredients till the mixture resembles coarse crumbs. Use solid shortening in biscuit making, rather than cooking oil or melted shortening. The best utensils for cutting in the solid shortening include a pastry blender, two knives, or a blending fork. Or, work the mixture together with your fingers until crumbly. However, work quickly since the warmth of the hands tends to soften the fat, making a sticky, difficult-to-handle mixture.

Make a well in the center of the crumbly mixture and add the liquid all at once. Buttermilk or sour milk is sometimes used instead of sweet milk. Stir the mixture quickly with a fork just till the dough follows fork around bowl and forms a soft dough.

Then, turn the dough out onto a lightly floured surface and knead gently 10 to 12 strokes. These kneading strokes help to develop the gluten and also aid in distributing the moisture evenly. For ease in kneading, curve your fingers over the dough, pull the dough toward you, then push it down and away from you with the heel of your hand. Give the dough a quarter turn, folding the dough toward you, and push it down again. Repeat this kneading motion for the number of strokes specified in the recipe.

Roll or pat the dough to ½-inch thickness. Then, cut the dough with a biscuit cutter. It's important to press the cutter straight down through the dough to get straight-sided, evenly shaped biscuits. Avoid twisting the cutter or flattening the cut biscuit edges. Be sure to dip the cutter in flour between each cut to prevent dough from sticking. Reroll scraps of dough and cut into biscuits. The recipe yields in this section include rerolls.

Another way of cutting biscuits is to roll the dough into a square or rectangle. Use a sharp knife to cut the dough into squares, triangles, or rectangles.

Carefully place biscuits on ungreased baking sheet. For crusty-sided biscuits, place the biscuits about 1 inch apart on baking sheet. For soft-sided biscuits, bake the biscuits close together in a baking pan.

The perfectly baked biscuit is uniform, straight-sided, and fairly smooth-topped with a golden brown top and a tender crust. The biscuit doubles in size as it bakes.

The inside appearance of a perfect biscuit varies, depending upon the type of biscuit prepared. A warm, flaky baking powder biscuit that is split open reveals a creamy white color, free from yellow or brown spots. The flaky biscuit enables you to pull off thin sheets of biscuit. Southern-style biscuits will have a creamy white color and a soft, tender crumb.

Serve baking powder biscuits piping hot from the oven with butter and honey, jam, or your favorite spread. Another popular way to serve biscuits is as a base for shortcakes.

Baking Powder Biscuits

2 cups all-purpose flour* *1 c.*
1 tablespoon baking powder* *1/2 tbsp*
½ teaspoon salt* *1/4*
⅓ cup shortening *2 1/2 tbsp*
¾ cup milk — *6 tbsp*

In bowl stir together flour, baking powder, and salt. Cut in shortening till mixture resembles coarse crumbs. Make a well in dry mixture; add milk all at once. Stir with fork just till dough clings together. Knead gently on lightly floured surface (10 to 12 strokes). Roll or pat dough to ½-inch thickness. Cut with 2½-inch biscuit cutter; dip cutter in flour between cuts. Bake on ungreased baking sheet at 450° till golden, about 12 minutes. Makes 10.

Note: When substituting self-rising all-purpose flour, omit the baking powder and salt.

Buttermilk Biscuits: Prepare Baking Powder Biscuits as above *except* add ¼ teaspoon baking soda to the flour mixture and substitute buttermilk for milk in recipe.

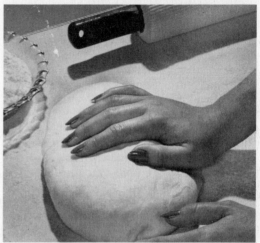

Bacon Biscuits: Crisp-cook 6 slices bacon; drain, reserving 2 tablespoons drippings. Crumble bacon; set aside. Prepare Baking Powder Biscuits as above *except* decrease shortening to ¼ cup. Add crumbled bacon, bacon drippings, and 2 teaspoons prepared horseradish along with milk.

Sour Cream Biscuits: Prepare Baking Powder Biscuits as above *except* substitute 1 cup dairy sour cream for the milk.

Shown top right: Prepare biscuits by stirring the dry ingredients together in a bowl. Cut in the shortening with a pastry blender, two knives, or blending fork, or use your fingers to work in the shortening until mixture resembles coarse crumbs. Make a well in center of dry mixture; add liquid all at once. Stir quickly till dough clings together. **Middle:** Turn dough onto a lightly floured surface; knead gently with palms of hands for 10 to 12 strokes. Pat or roll dough to ½-inch thickness. **Bottom:** Cut standard size biscuits with a 2- to 2½-inch biscuit cutter or tea-size biscuits with a 1- to 1½-inch cutter. Dip cutter in flour before cutting and between cuts.

Popular Biscuits

Cheddar Cheese Biscuits

Cheesy biscuits topped with crunchy seeds—

  2 cups all-purpose flour
  1 tablespoon baking powder
  ½ teaspoon salt
  ¼ cup shortening
  • • •
  1 beaten egg
  ¾ cup milk
  ½ cup shredded sharp Cheddar
    cheese (2 ounces)
  1 tablespoon butter *or* margarine,
    melted
    Poppy seed *or* sesame seed

In mixing bowl thoroughly stir together the flour, baking powder, and salt. Cut in shortening till mixture resembles coarse crumbs. Make a well in center of dry mixture. Combine egg and milk; add all at once to dry mixture. Add shredded cheese. Stir just till dough clings together. Knead gently on lightly floured surface (10 to 12 strokes). Roll or pat dough to ½-inch thickness. Cut with 2½-inch biscuit cutter; dip cutter in flour between cuts. Place on ungreased baking sheet. Brush tops with melted butter or margarine. Sprinkle with poppy or sesame seed. Bake at 450° for 10 to 12 minutes. Makes 10 biscuits.

Buttermilk Pan Biscuits

Mix up the dough, pinch off a piece, and roll it into balls. No biscuit cutter is needed—

  ¼ cup lard
  2 cups self-rising all-purpose
    flour
  ¾ cup buttermilk

In mixing bowl cut lard into flour until mixture resembles coarse crumbs. Make a well in the center; add buttermilk all at once. Stir quickly with fork just till dough clings together. Divide dough in eighths. Form each piece into a ball. Place in greased 9-inch pie plate. Press to flatten tops. Bake at 450° for 12 to 15 minutes. Makes 8 biscuits.

Biscuits Supreme

Good to use as a base for shortcake—

  2 cups all-purpose flour
  4 teaspoons baking powder
  2 teaspoons sugar
  ½ teaspoon cream of tartar
  ½ cup shortening
  ⅔ cup milk

Stir together the flour, baking powder, sugar, cream of tartar, and ½ teaspoon salt. Cut in shortening till mixture resembles coarse crumbs. Make a well in center; add milk all at once. Stir just till dough clings together. Knead gently on lightly floured surface (10 to 12 strokes). Roll or pat dough to ½-inch thickness. Cut with 2½-inch biscuit cutter; dip cutter in flour between cuts. Bake on ungreased baking sheet at 450° for 10 to 12 minutes. Makes 10.

Cornmeal Biscuits

  1½ cups all-purpose flour
  ½ cup yellow cornmeal
  1 tablespoon baking powder
  ⅓ cup shortening
  1 cup milk

Stir together flour, cornmeal, baking powder, and ½ teaspoon salt. Cut in shortening till mixture resembles coarse crumbs. Make a well in dry mixture; add milk all at once. Stir just till dough clings together. (Dough will be very soft.) Knead gently on well-floured surface (10 to 12 strokes). Roll or pat dough to ½-inch thickness. Cut with 2½-inch biscuit cutter; dip cutter in flour between cuts. Place on ungreased baking sheet. Bake at 450° till golden, 10 to 12 minutes. Makes 10 biscuits.

Nothing could compliment the cook or the ▶ meal more than high, flaky *Baking Powder Biscuits* (see recipe, page 49). Perfect anytime, biscuits should be served piping hot with plenty of butter and the family's favorite preserves.

Garden-Fresh Biscuits

Laced with bits of parsley, carrot, and onion—

- **2 cups all-purpose flour**
- **1 tablespoon baking powder**
- **½ teaspoon salt**
- **6 tablespoons butter *or* margarine**
- **2 tablespoons finely chopped carrot**
- **1 tablespoon finely chopped parsley**
- **1 teaspoon finely chopped green onion**
- **¾ cup milk**

In mixing bowl thoroughly stir together the flour, baking powder, and salt. Cut in butter or margarine till mixture resembles coarse crumbs. Stir in carrot, parsley, and green onion. Make a well in dry mixture; add milk all at once. Stir just till dough clings together. Knead gently on lightly floured surface (10 to 12 strokes). Roll or pat dough to ½-inch thickness. Cut with 2½-inch biscuit cutter; dip cutter in flour between cuts. Place on ungreased baking sheet. Bake at 450° for 10 to 12 minutes. Makes 10 biscuits.

Sweet Potato Biscuits

These golden biscuits, delicately flavored with sweet potato, are seen on pages 46 and 47—

- **1¼ cups all-purpose flour**
- **1 tablespoon baking powder**
- **2 teaspoons packed brown sugar**
- **½ teaspoon salt**
- **⅓ cup shortening**

- **• • •**

- **1 beaten egg**
- **½ cup mashed, cooked sweet potato**
- **2 tablespoons milk**

In mixing bowl stir together the flour, baking powder, brown sugar, and salt. Cut in shortening till mixture resembles coarse crumbs. Combine egg, mashed sweet potato, and milk; add all at once to dry mixture. Stir just till dough clings together. Knead gently on lightly floured surface (10 to 12 strokes). Roll or pat dough to ½-inch thickness. Cut with 2½-inch biscuit cutter; dip cutter in flour between cuts. Place on ungreased baking sheet. Bake at 425° for 10 to 12 minutes. Makes 8 biscuits.

Beer Biscuits

Thoroughly stir together 2 cups packaged biscuit mix and ½ cup shredded Cheddar cheese (2 ounces). Make a well in center; add ½ cup beer all at once. Stir just till dough clings together. Knead gently on lightly floured surface (5 strokes). Roll or pat dough to a rectangle 3½ inches wide and ½ inch thick. Cut into triangles. Place on ungreased baking sheet. Bake at 450° for 8 to 10 minutes. Makes 10 biscuits.

Sunflower Seed Biscuits

- **1½ cups all-purpose flour**
- **½ cup whole wheat flour**
- **4 teaspoons baking powder**
- **1 tablespoon sugar**
- **½ cup shortening**
- **¼ cup chopped shelled sunflower seed**
- **⅔ cup dairy sour cream**
- **¼ cup milk**

Thoroughly stir together both flours, baking powder, sugar, and ½ teaspoon salt. Cut in shortening till mixture resembles coarse crumbs. Stir in *2 tablespoons* of the sunflower seed. Make a well in center. Combine sour cream and milk; add all at once to dry mixture. Stir just till dough clings together. Knead gently on lightly floured surface (10 to 12 strokes). Roll or pat to ½-inch thickness. Cut with 2½-inch biscuit cutter. Place on greased baking sheet. Brush tops with a little milk. Sprinkle with remaining sunflower seed. Bake at 450° for 10 to 12 minutes. Makes 12 biscuits.

Taco Biscuits

In small bowl combine ¼ cup sauce for tacos (½ of a 4-ounce can), ¼ cup milk, and ½ teaspoon instant minced onion; let stand 5 minutes. Stir in 2 cups packaged biscuit mix till dough clings together. Knead gently on lightly floured surface (5 strokes). Roll or pat dough to ½-inch thickness. Cut with 2½-inch biscuit cutter. Brush with melted butter. Sprinkle with 2 tablespoons grated Parmesan cheese. Bake on ungreased baking sheet at 450° for 8 to 10 minutes. Makes 8 to 10 biscuits.

Buttermilk-Bran Scones

This nutritious muffin would taste great with steaming hot cocoa —

½ cup dried currants *or* raisins,
    chopped
2 cups all-purpose flour
¼ cup sugar
1 tablespoon baking powder
1 teaspoon salt
½ teaspoon baking soda
¼ cup butter *or* margarine
2 cups bran flakes
2 beaten eggs
⅓ cup buttermilk *or* sour milk

In small bowl pour boiling water over currants or raisins to cover. Let stand 5 minutes; drain well. In mixing bowl thoroughly stir together flour, sugar, baking powder, salt, and baking soda. Cut in butter or margarine till mixture resembles coarse crumbs. Stir in bran flakes and drained currants or raisins.

Combine eggs and buttermilk or sour milk; add all at once to dry ingredients. Stir till dough clings together. Knead gently on lightly floured surface (5 or 6 strokes). Divide dough in half. Roll or pat *each* half to 7-inch circle, ½ inch thick. Cut each circle in 6 wedges. Place on greased baking sheet. Bake at 400° for 12 to 15 minutes. Makes 12 scones.

Oatmeal-Currant Scones

Serve these warm with cold mugs of milk —

1 cup all-purpose flour
3 tablespoons sugar
2 teaspoons baking powder
¼ teaspoon salt
6 tablespoons butter *or* margarine
1 cup quick-cooking rolled oats
½ cup dried currants
2 beaten eggs

In mixing bowl thoroughly stir together flour, sugar, baking powder, and salt. Cut in butter or margarine till mixture resembles coarse crumbs. Stir in oats and currants. Stir in eggs till dry ingredients are moistened. On lightly floured surface roll or pat dough to 7-inch circle, ½ inch thick. Cut circle in 12 wedges. Place on greased baking sheet. Bake at 400° for 10 to 12 minutes. Makes 12 scones.

Whole Wheat-Granola Scones

These are hearty and full of great flavors — honey, whole wheat, and granola with raisins and dates —

1½ cups all-purpose flour
½ cup whole wheat flour
4 teaspoons baking powder
½ teaspoon salt
¼ cup shortening
2 cups granola cereal with
    raisins and dates
2 beaten eggs
⅓ cup milk
¼ cup honey

In mixing bowl thoroughly stir together all-purpose flour, whole wheat flour, baking powder, and salt. Cut in shortening till mixture resembles coarse crumbs. Stir in granola cereal. Combine eggs, milk, and honey; stir into dry ingredients till dough clings together.

Knead gently on lightly floured surface (5 or 6 strokes). (Dough may be slightly sticky.) Divide dough in half. Roll or pat *each* half to 7-inch circle, ½ inch thick. Cut each circle in 6 wedges. Place on greased baking sheet. Bake at 400° for 12 to 15 minutes. Makes 12 scones.

Oatcakes

Serve crispy oatmeal wedges with lots of butter —

1 cup quick-cooking rolled oats
2 tablespoons all-purpose flour
¼ teaspoon baking powder
¼ teaspoon salt
2 tablespoons butter *or* margarine,
    melted
¼ cup hot water
¼ cup quick-cooking rolled oats

Place ½ *cup* of the oats in blender container; cover and blend till oats are a fine powder. Repeat with another ½ *cup* oats. Combine blended oats, flour, baking powder, and salt. Stir in melted butter. Blend in hot water. Sprinkle a board with ¼ cup oats. Roll dough in oatmeal to cover surface of dough. Roll dough to a 10-inch circle, about ⅛ inch thick. Cut into 12 wedges. Place on ungreased baking sheet. Bake at 350° for 15 minutes. Turn off heat and open oven door. Leave oatcakes in oven till firm and crisp, 4 to 5 minutes. Serve with butter. Makes 12 oatcakes.

Just-for-Fun Biscuits

Sesame Swirls

2½ cups all-purpose flour
1 tablespoon baking powder
½ cup butter *or* margarine
1 cup dairy sour cream
½ cup milk
1 slightly beaten egg
⅓ cup sesame seed, toasted

Stir together flour, baking powder, and 1 teaspoon salt. Cut in butter till mixture resembles coarse crumbs. Stir sour cream and milk together. Add all at once to dry mixture. Stir just till dough clings together. Knead gently on lightly floured surface (10 to 12 strokes). Roll dough to 15x12-inch rectangle. Brush with some of the egg. Sprinkle with sesame seed. Roll up jelly-roll fashion, starting with long side. Cut into 18 slices; place on greased baking sheet. Brush tops with remaining egg. Bake at 425° about 15 minutes. Makes 18.

Pineapple-Cheese Biscuit Balls

1 8¼-ounce can pineapple tidbits
1 3-ounce package cream cheese, cut into 16 pieces
2 tablespoons sugar
1 teaspoon ground cinnamon
2 cups packaged biscuit mix
¼ cup sugar
⅓ cup milk
1 tablespoon milk

Pat 16 pineapple tidbits dry on paper toweling (reserve remaining tidbits for another use). Press one tidbit into each piece of cream cheese; set aside. Combine the 2 tablespoons sugar and cinnamon; set aside. In mixing bowl stir together the biscuit mix and ¼ cup sugar. Add ⅓ cup milk all at once, stirring till dough clings together. Divide into 16 portions. Shape each piece of dough around one cream cheese piece to form a ball. Brush balls with the 1 tablespoon milk. Dip balls in sugar-cinnamon mixture. Place on greased baking sheet. Bake at 425° for 12 to 15 minutes. Makes 16.

Pecan Spirals

Serve these large biscuit twists for breakfast or as a hearty snack—

2 cups all-purpose flour
2 tablespoons granulated sugar
1 tablespoon baking powder
½ teaspoon salt
½ cup butter *or* margarine
1 beaten egg
½ cup milk
1 tablespoon butter *or* margarine, melted
3 tablespoons finely chopped pecans
3 tablespoons packed brown sugar *or* granulated sugar
1 cup sifted powdered sugar
4 to 5 teaspoons milk

In mixing bowl thoroughly stir together the flour, 2 tablespoons granulated sugar, baking powder, and salt. Cut in the ½ cup butter or margarine till mixture resembles coarse crumbs. Make a well in center of dry ingredients. Combine beaten egg and milk; add all at once to dry mixture. Stir just till dough clings together. Knead gently on lightly floured surface (12 to 15 strokes).

Roll or pat dough to 15x8-inch rectangle. Brush with 1 tablespoon melted butter. Combine pecans and 3 tablespoons brown or granulated sugar; sprinkle over dough. Fold dough in half lengthwise to make a 15x4-inch rectangle. Cut in 1-inch strips. Holding strip at both ends, twist in opposite directions twice, forming a spiral. Place spirals on lightly greased baking sheet pressing both ends down. Bake at 450° about 10 minutes. Combine powdered sugar and 4 to 5 teaspoons milk till of drizzling consistency. Drizzle over spirals. Makes 15.

Mix up some biscuit dough and have fun making spirals, swirls, balls, and other shapes of your own. Shaped biscuits, such as *Sesame Swirls* and *Pecan Spirals*, not only are enjoyable to make but taste great, too.

Drop biscuit dough has a softer consistency than the dough for standard biscuits because more liquid is added. To shape the dough, drop rounded spoonfuls onto greased baking sheets or into muffin pans. The top of a baked drop biscuit is pebbly in appearance.

Drop Biscuits

      2 cups all-purpose flour
      1 tablespoon baking powder
   ⅓ cup shortening
      1 cup milk

Stir together the flour, baking powder, and ½ teaspoon salt. Cut in shortening till mixture resembles coarse crumbs. Make a well in dry mixture; add milk all at once. Stir just till dough clings together. Drop from table-spoon onto greased baking sheet. Bake at 450° about 12 minutes. Makes 12 to 14 biscuits.

Mayonnaise Drop Biscuits

      2 cups self-rising all-purpose
         flour
   ⅛ teaspoon cayenne
   ⅔ cup milk
   ½ cup mayonnaise *or* salad dressing

Stir flour and cayenne together. Add milk and mayonnaise. Stir till dough clings together. Drop from tablespoon onto ungreased baking sheet. Brush with additional milk, if desired. Bake at 450° for 10 to 12 minutes. Makes 12.

Mini Raisin Drop Biscuits

Freeze extra biscuits, baked in muffin pans, for later use. Heat biscuits before serving—

      4 cups all-purpose flour
   ½ cup sugar
      2 tablespoons baking powder
      2 teaspoons salt
   ⅔ cup shortening
      2 cups raisins
      1 teaspoon grated orange peel
      2 beaten eggs
   1½ cups milk
                 • • •
      2 tablespoons butter *or* margarine,
         melted
      3 tablespoons sugar
   ¼ teaspoon ground cinnamon
   ⅛ teaspoon ground nutmeg

Thoroughly stir together the flour, ½ cup sugar, baking powder, and salt. Cut in shortening till mixture resembles coarse crumbs. Stir in raisins and peel. Combine eggs and milk; add all at once to dry mixture. Stir quickly just till dough clings together. Drop from teaspoon into greased 1¾-inch muffin pans filling pans ⅔ full. Bake at 400° for 15 to 20 minutes. While biscuits are warm, dip tops in melted butter and then in a mixture of 3 tablespoons sugar, cinnamon, and nutmeg. Makes 48.

Whole Wheat Drop Biscuit

Wholesome biscuits seen on pages 46 and 47—

      1 cup all-purpose flour
      1 cup whole wheat flour
      1 tablespoon baking powder
   ½ teaspoon salt
                 • • •
   ⅓ cup shortening
   ¼ cup shelled sunflower seed
      1 beaten egg
      1 cup milk

Thoroughly stir together the flours, baking powder, and salt. Cut in shortening till mix-ture resembles coarse crumbs. Stir in sun-flower seed. Combine egg and milk; add all at once to dry mixture. Stir quickly just till dough clings together. Drop from tablespoon onto ungreased baking sheet. Bake at 450° for 12 to 15 minutes. Makes 12 to 14 biscuits.

Apple Drop Biscuits

   2 cups packaged biscuit mix
   ¼ cup chopped walnuts
   2 tablespoons sugar
   ¾ teaspoon apple pie spice
   ½ cup apple cider *or* apple juice
   ½ cup shredded peeled apple

Stir together biscuit mix, walnuts, sugar, and apple pie spice. Add cider and apple, stirring just till dough clings together. Drop from tablespoon onto greased baking sheet. Bake at 450° for 10 to 12 minutes. Makes 12 biscuits.

Pecan Petal Biscuits

Frosted biscuits shown on pages 46 and 47 —

   1⅔ cups all-purpose flour
   ¼ cup granulated sugar
   2 teaspoons baking powder
   ½ teaspoon baking soda
   ½ teaspoon cream of tartar
   ½ teaspoon salt
       • • •
   ⅓ cup shortening
   ½ cup chopped pecans
   1 beaten egg
   ½ cup buttermilk
   2 tablespoons butter *or* margarine,
       melted
       • • •
   ½ cup sifted powdered sugar
   ½ teaspoon vanilla
   Milk

Stir together the flour, granulated sugar, baking powder, soda, cream of tartar, and salt. Cut in shortening till mixture resembles coarse crumbs. Stir in pecans. Combine egg and buttermilk; add all at once to dry mixture. Stir just till dough clings together. Knead gently on lightly floured surface (10 to 12 strokes). Roll to 15x10-inch rectangle. Brush with melted butter. Cut crosswise into ten 10x1½-inch strips. Make 2 stacks of 5 strips each. Cut each stack in 6 pieces. Place biscuits, 1½-inch side down, in greased muffin pans. Bake at 400° about 22 minutes.

Meanwhile, in small bowl combine the powdered sugar and vanilla. Stir in enough milk (about 1½ teaspoons) till of drizzling consistency. Drizzle over warm biscuits. Makes 12.

To make petal biscuits, stack strips of dough in two piles; cut each stack in six pieces. Place biscuit stacks in greased muffin pans.

Rhubarb Sticky Buns

   2 cups all-purpose flour
   3 tablespoons sugar
   4 teaspoons baking powder
   ½ teaspoon cream of tartar
   ½ teaspoon salt
   ½ cup shortening
   ½ cup milk
   1 tablespoon butter *or* margarine,
       melted
   2 cups finely diced rhubarb
   ¾ cup sugar
   1 teaspoon grated orange peel

In mixing bowl stir together flour, 3 tablespoons sugar, baking powder, cream of tartar, and salt. Cut in shortening till mixture resembles coarse crumbs. Make a well in dry mixture; add milk all at once, stirring just till dough clings together. Knead gently on lightly floured surface (10 to 12 strokes).

Roll dough to 12x10-inch rectangle. Brush with melted butter or margarine. Combine diced rhubarb, ¾ cup sugar, and orange peel. Spread over dough. Roll up, jelly-roll fashion, starting from long side; seal edge. Cut in 1-inch slices. Arrange slices in greased 9x9x2-inch baking pan. Bake at 425° for 25 to 30 minutes. Cool in pan 5 minutes; turn out of pan. Serve warm. Makes 12 rolls.

Daisy Biscuits

Find these flower-shaped biscuits on page 2 —

> **2 cups all-purpose flour**
> **1 tablespoon baking powder**
> **¼ cup butter** *or* **margarine**
> **1 3-ounce package cream cheese**
> **¾ cup milk**
> **1 stiffly beaten egg white**
> **2 tablespoons orange marmalade** *or* **raspberry jam**

Stir together flour, baking powder, and ½ teaspoon salt. Cut in butter and cream cheese till mixture is crumbly. Add milk all at once. Stir just till dough clings together. Knead gently on lightly floured surface (4 or 5 strokes).

Roll or pat dough to slightly less than ½-inch thickness. Cut with floured 2½-inch biscuit cutter. To make daisy design, make 6 slits through dough around edge of each, to within ¼ inch of center. Place on ungreased baking sheet. Press down center of each biscuit with thumb. Brush biscuits with egg white. Spoon ½ *teaspoon* marmalade into *each* biscuit center. Bake at 450° for 10 to 12 minutes. Makes 12.

Shape tasty *Cinnamon Twists* from refrigerated biscuit dough for easy snacks. Use your imagination to concoct other interesting shapes.

Butter Logs

Rich, buttery flavor of these biscuit sticks makes them the perfect mate for fresh, green salads —

> **2 cups all-purpose flour**
> **3 tablespoons toasted sesame seed**
> **1 tablespoon sugar**
> **2½ teaspoons baking powder**
> **½ teaspoon cream of tartar**
> **½ teaspoon salt**
> • • •
> **¼ cup shortening**
> **2 beaten eggs**
> **½ cup milk**
> **¼ cup butter** *or* **margarine, melted**

In mixing bowl stir together the flour, sesame seed, sugar, baking powder, cream of tartar, and salt. Cut in shortening till mixture resembles coarse crumbs. Combine eggs and milk; add all at once to dry mixture. Stir just till dough clings together. Knead gently on lightly floured surface (10 to 12 strokes).

Roll or pat dough to 10x6-inch rectangle. With floured knife, cut dough in half lengthwise. Then cut each half crosswise into eight 3-inch sticks. Place *1 tablespoon* of the butter or margarine in 13x9x2-inch baking pan. Place sticks in pan; brush with remaining butter or margarine. Bake at 425° till light brown, 18 to 20 minutes. Makes 16 butter logs.

Cinnamon Twists

Quick-to-fix with either refrigerated biscuits or Baking Powder Biscuits (see recipe, page 49) —

> **1 package refrigerated biscuits (8 biscuits)**
> **2 tablespoons butter** *or* **margarine, melted**
> **¼ cup sugar**
> **1 teaspoon ground cinnamon**
> **1 tablespoon chopped walnuts**

Roll each biscuit between hands to form a 9-inch rope. Pinch ends together to form a circle. Dip biscuit circles in melted butter, then in mixture of sugar and cinnamon. Twist each biscuit to form a figure 8. Place biscuits on ungreased baking sheet. Sprinkle with chopped walnuts. Bake at 425° for 8 to 10 minutes. Makes 8 twists.

Shortcut Beaten Biscuits

2 cups self-rising all-purpose
    flour
1 tablespoon sugar
¼ cup shortening

In bowl stir together flour and sugar. Cut in shortening till mixture resembles coarse crumbs. Add ⅔ cup water, a little at a time, stirring to make a stiff dough. Knead on lightly floured surface (15 to 20 strokes). Pound dough with flat side of mallet 2 to 3 minutes. Roll or pat dough to ½-inch thickness. Cut with 2-inch biscuit cutter; dip cutter in flour between cuts. Place on ungreased baking sheet. Prick tops with fork. Bake at 400° till lightly browned, about 20 minutes. Makes 18.

Self-rising flour makes *Shortcut Beaten Biscuits* a speedy variation of the old-time favorite. The cracker-like biscuit is typically pricked with a fork before baking.

Shortcake

2 cups all-purpose flour
2 tablespoons sugar
1 tablespoon baking powder
½ cup butter *or* margarine
1 beaten egg
⅔ cup light cream

Stir together flour, sugar, baking powder, and ½ teaspoon salt. Cut in butter till mixture resembles coarse crumbs. Combine egg and cream; add all at once to dry mixture, stirring just till moistened. Spread dough in greased 8x8x2-inch baking pan, building up edges slightly. Bake at 450° for 15 to 18 minutes. Remove from pan; cool. Split in half horizontally; fill and top with fruit and whipped cream.

Bacon Biscuit Bars

Cheese and bacon bars shown on pages 46 and 47—

Stir together 2 cups packaged biscuit mix, ½ cup shredded sharp American cheese (2 ounces), and 6 slices bacon, crisp-cooked, drained, and crumbled. Add ½ cup cold water, stirring just till dough clings together. Knead gently on lightly floured surface (5 strokes).

Roll or pat dough to 10x6-inch rectangle. Cut with floured knife into six 10x1-inch strips. Cut each strip into thirds. Bake on ungreased baking sheet at 450° till golden, about 10 minutes. Makes 18 biscuits.

Party Biscuit Foldovers

Filled with Cheddar cheese and sour cream—

1 cup all-purpose flour
1 teaspoon baking powder
¼ teaspoon baking soda
¼ teaspoon salt
• • •
2 tablespoons shortening
1 beaten egg
⅓ cup dairy sour cream
¼ cup shredded Cheddar cheese
    (1 ounce)
3 tablespoons dairy sour cream

In mixing bowl thoroughly stir together the flour, baking powder, baking soda, and salt. Cut in shortening till mixture resembles coarse crumbs. Combine egg and ⅓ cup dairy sour cream. Stir into dry mixture just till dough clings together. Knead gently on lightly floured surface (10 to 12 strokes).

Roll or pat dough to ¼-inch thickness; cut with floured 2½-inch biscuit cutter. Crease biscuit just off-center with back of knife. Stir together Cheddar cheese and the 3 tablespoons sour cream. Place *1 teaspoon* filling on smaller half of *each* biscuit; fold so larger half overlaps slightly. Seal end edges of each biscuit. Bake on ungreased baking sheet at 425° for 8 to 10 minutes. Makes 12 biscuits.

Quick Bread Assortment

Remember that coffee cakes, nut breads, muffins, and biscuits are only the beginning of the quick bread roster. Add to that list doughnuts, fritters, pancakes, waffles, dumplings, popovers, and French toast. That's still only a start because the possibilities for you to discover and enjoy are endless.

Chock-full of taste-tempting recipes, this last section gives you a wide array of the remaining quick bread types, from those that round out the meal to those that star as the entrée. In addition, helpful tips and pictures are included to aid you with the various quick breads.

Be sure to look in this section for quick and easy recipes that turn convenience products into your own home-baked specialties.

This is a sampling of the types of quick breads found in this section: *Cinnamon-Graham Crackers, Cheesy Spoon Bread, Apricot-Sauced Pecan Waffles, Poppy Seed Crescent Loaf,* and *Spicy Spud Doughnuts.* (See Index for page numbers.)

Doughnuts and Fritters

Nothing whets the appetite like freshly fried doughnuts or fritters. While both are deep-fat fried, fritters are made with a batter and contain a fruit or vegetable; doughnuts are made with a sweetened, leavened dough and are popular as breakfast or snack-time treats.

Proper measuring of ingredients and preparation of the dough or batter are particularly important for producing light-textured doughnuts and fritters. There are, however, a few special preparation techniques to keep in mind when making doughnuts. If necessary, chill the dough to make rolling and cutting easier. And, be sure to use as little flour as possible when rolling out the dough. Avoid overhandling—excessive handling makes doughnuts tough.

Correct frying techniques are essential to both doughnuts and fritters. Fry until the underside is browned, then turn once and cook till the other side also is browned evenly. Fry only a few doughnuts or fritters at a time for best results. If too many are fried at once, the fat temperature will drop causing the product to cook slowly and become fat-soaked.

Coconut Cake Doughnuts

    2⅓ cups all-purpose flour
     2 teaspoons baking powder
     2 beaten eggs
    ½ cup sugar
    ¼ cup milk
     2 tablespoons shortening, melted
    ¾ cup flaked coconut
       Fat for frying

Stir together the flour, baking powder, and ½ teaspoon salt. Beat eggs and sugar together till thick and lemon-colored. Stir in milk and cooled shortening. Add dry ingredients and coconut to egg mixture, stirring just till blended. Cover; chill several hours. Roll out on lightly floured surface to ½-inch thickness. Cut with floured 2½-inch doughnut cutter. Fry in deep hot fat (375°) about 1 minute per side, turning once. Drain on paper toweling. Dust with sugar, if desired. Makes 12 doughnuts.

Cake Doughnuts

    3¼ cups all-purpose flour
     2 teaspoons baking powder
     1 teaspoon ground cinnamon
    ¼ teaspoon ground nutmeg
     2 beaten eggs
    ⅔ cup sugar
     1 teaspoon vanilla
    ⅔ cup light cream
    ¼ cup butter or margarine, melted
       Fat for frying
    ½ cup sugar

In bowl stir together the flour, baking powder, ½ *teaspoon* of the cinnamon, nutmeg, and dash salt. Beat eggs, ⅔ cup sugar, and vanilla together till thick and lemon-colored. Combine cream and butter; add dry ingredients and cream mixture alternately to egg mixture. Beat just till blended after each addition. Cover and chill dough about 2 hours.

Roll dough out on lightly floured surface to ⅜-inch thickness. Cut with floured 2½-inch doughnut cutter. Fry in deep hot fat (375°) till golden brown, about 1 minute per side, turning once. Drain on paper toweling. While warm, shake in mixture of ½ cup sugar and remaining ½ teaspoon cinnamon. Makes 20.

Baked Doughnut Twists

Combine 2 cups packaged biscuit mix and 2 tablespoons sugar. Dissolve 1 teaspoon instant coffee granules in ¼ cup milk; stir in 1 beaten egg and 1 teaspoon grated orange peel. Add mixture to dry ingredients; stir just till moistened. Knead on well-floured surface (10 to 12 strokes). Roll to ½-inch thickness. Cut with floured 2½-inch doughnut cutter. Holding opposite sides of doughnut, stretch and twist to form a figure eight. Bake on ungreased baking sheet at 400° for 10 to 12 minutes. Brush liberally with melted butter; coat with a mixture of ½ cup sugar, 1 teaspoon ground cinnamon, and ¼ teaspoon ground nutmeg. Serve warm. Makes 8 doughnuts.

Buttermilk Doughnuts

4 cups all-purpose flour
4 teaspoons baking powder
¾ teaspoon salt
¼ teaspoon baking soda
2 beaten eggs
1 cup granulated sugar
¼ cup cooking oil
1 teaspoon vanilla
1 cup buttermilk

• • •

Fat for frying
Sifted powdered sugar

In bowl stir together the flour, baking powder, salt, and baking soda. Beat eggs and granulated sugar together till thick and lemon-colored. Stir in oil and vanilla. Add dry ingredients and buttermilk alternately to egg mixture, beginning and ending with dry ingredients. Beat just till blended after each addition. Roll dough out on lightly floured surface to ½-inch thickness. Cut with floured 2½-inch doughnut cutter. Fry in deep hot fat (375°) till golden brown, about 1½ minutes per side, turning once. Drain. Sprinkle with powdered sugar. Makes 24.

Shown top right: Roll chilled doughnut dough to thickness specified in recipe. Cut dough with doughnut cutter. Push cutter through dough straight down without twisting. Dip the cutter in flour between cuts. Allow baking powder leavened doughnuts to stand for a few minutes before frying so that a delicate, thin crust will form. This thin crust retards the immediate absorption of fat. **Middle:** The temperature of the fat for frying doughnuts is extremely important to the finished product. (Use a thermometer specially made for deep-fat frying.) The temperature of the fat should be between 350° and 375°. If the fat temperature is too low, the doughnut will become soaked with fat. When the temperature is too hot, the doughnut will cook too fast on the outside, leaving an uncooked center. Turn the doughnuts with a fork or slotted spoon after they have risen to the top so that both sides brown evenly. **Bottom:** Remove doughnuts from the hot fat with a slotted spoon or fork. Place the doughnuts on a rack covered with paper toweling to drain and cool.

Chocolate-Cinnamon Doughnuts

  4 cups all-purpose flour
  ⅓ cup unsweetened cocoa powder
  4 teaspoons baking powder
  1 teaspoon ground cinnamon
  ¾ teaspoon salt
  ¼ teaspoon baking soda
     • • •
  2 beaten eggs
  1¼ cups sugar
  ¼ cup cooking oil
  1 teaspoon vanilla
  ¾ cup buttermilk
     Fat for frying
     Cinnamon Glaze

In bowl stir together the flour, cocoa powder, baking powder, cinnamon, salt, and baking soda. Beat eggs and sugar together till thick and lemon-colored. Stir in oil and vanilla. Add dry ingredients and buttermilk alternately to egg mixture, beginning and ending with dry ingredients. Beat just till blended after each addition. Chill dough about 2 hours.

Roll dough on lightly floured surface, half at a time, to ½-inch thickness. (Keep remaining dough chilled.) Cut with floured 2½-inch cutter. Fry in deep hot fat (375°) about 1½ minutes per side; turn once. Drain. Dip warm doughnuts in Cinnamon Glaze. Makes 24.

Cinnamon Glaze: In small mixing bowl combine 4 cups sifted powdered sugar, 1 teaspoon vanilla, ½ teaspoon ground cinnamon, and enough milk to make of spreading consistency.

Apple Fritter Rings

Core and peel 4 large tart apples; cut into ½-inch-thick rings. In mixing bowl thoroughly stir together 1 cup all-purpose flour, 2 tablespoons sugar, 1 teaspoon baking powder, and dash salt. Combine 1 beaten egg, ⅔ cup milk, and 1 teaspoon cooking oil; add all at once to dry ingredients stirring just till blended. Heat 1 inch cooking oil to 375° in skillet that is at least 2 inches deep. Dip apple slices in batter one at a time. Fry fritters in hot oil till brown, about 1½ minutes per side, turning once. Drain on paper toweling. Sprinkle warm fritters with a mixture of ¼ cup sugar and ½ teaspoon ground cinnamon. Serve hot. Makes 16.

Orange Doughnuts

  3¼ cups all-purpose flour
  2 teaspoons baking powder
  2 beaten eggs
  ⅔ cup sugar
  1 teaspoon vanilla
  1 teaspoon grated orange peel
  ⅔ cup orange juice
  ¼ cup butter *or* margarine, melted
     Fat for frying
     Orange Glaze

Stir together flour, baking powder, and dash salt. Beat eggs, sugar, and vanilla together till thick and lemon-colored. Combine orange peel, juice, and butter. Add orange mixture and ¾ of the dry ingredients alternately to egg mixture. Beat with electric mixer just till blended after each addition. Stir in remaining dry ingredients by hand. Cover; chill dough 2 hours. Roll dough on lightly floured surface to ⅜-inch thickness. Cut with floured 2½-inch doughnut cutter. Fry in deep hot fat (375°) about 1 minute per side, turning once. Drain on paper toweling. While warm, drizzle with Orange Glaze. Makes 16 doughnuts.

Orange Glaze: Stir together 2 cups sifted powdered sugar, 1 teaspoon grated orange peel, and 3 tablespoons orange juice.

Easy Raised Doughnuts

  1 loaf frozen white bread dough
     (1 pound)
     Fat for frying
     Glaze

Thaw bread and let rise till double in size. Roll dough on lightly floured surface to a 12x9-inch rectangle. Cut with floured 2½-inch doughnut cutter. Cover; let rise till almost double, about 1 hour. Fry in deep hot fat (365°) about 1 minute per side, turning once. Drain on paper toweling. Brush with Glaze. Makes 18.

Glaze: Mix 1 cup sifted powdered sugar, 4 teaspoons milk, and few drops almond extract.

Delicately flavored, tender *Orange Doughnuts* ▶ make an afternoon snack or morning brunch a memorable occasion. Fry and glaze the doughnut holes as well as the doughnuts.

Homemade specials include *Jiffy Grape Bismarcks, Cranberry-Orange Rumbas* (see recipe, page 34), and *Pecan Doughnut Balls.*

Spicy Spud Doughnuts

Delicate potato doughnuts seen on pages 60 and 61—

    4 cups all-purpose flour
    2 tablespoons baking powder
    ½ teaspoon ground cloves
    ½ teaspoon ground cinnamon
    3 beaten eggs
    1 cup packed brown sugar
 1½ cups mashed cooked potatoes
    2 tablespoons shortening, melted
    1 5⅓-ounce can evaporated milk
      Fat for frying

Stir together first 4 ingredients and 1 teaspoon salt. Beat eggs and sugar till thick. Stir in cooled potatoes, shortening, and milk. Gradually add dry ingredients to potato mixture, stirring till combined. Chill at least 3 hours. Roll dough on well-floured surface, half at a time, to ⅜-inch thickness. Cut with floured doughnut cutter; chill 15 minutes. Fry in deep hot fat (365°) for 1 to 1½ minutes per side, turning once. Drain. Makes 36 doughnuts.

Gingerbread Doughnut Twists

 2¾ cups all-purpose flour
    1 tablespoon baking powder
    2 teaspoons ground ginger
    ½ teaspoon baking soda
    2 eggs
    ½ cup packed brown sugar
    ½ cup dairy sour cream
    ¼ cup light molasses
    ¼ cup cooking oil
      Fat for frying
      Lemon Glaze

Stir together flour, baking powder, ginger, soda, and ½ teaspoon salt. Beat eggs till thick and lemon-colored; beat in sugar, sour cream, molasses, and cooking oil. Stir in dry ingredients just till moistened. Roll dough on lightly floured surface to 9-inch square. Cut into strips 1 inch wide. Cut each strip in half crosswise. Shape strips of dough into 12-inch ropes. Fold in half; twist several times. Pinch to secure ends. Fry in deep hot fat (375°) for 1 to 1½ minutes per side, turning once. Drain. Dip in Lemon Glaze. Makes 18.

    Lemon Glaze: Mix 2 cups sifted powdered sugar, 2 tablespoons milk, 1 teaspoon grated lemon peel, and 1 tablespoon lemon juice.

Pecan Doughnut Balls

    2 cups all-purpose flour
    ¼ cup sugar
    1 tablespoon baking powder
    1 teaspoon ground cinnamon
    ½ teaspoon ground nutmeg
    1 beaten egg
    ½ cup milk
    1 teaspoon grated orange peel
    ¼ cup orange juice
    ¼ cup cooking oil
    ¼ cup coarsely chopped pecans
      Fat for frying

Stir together flour, sugar, baking powder, spices, and 1 teaspoon salt. Combine egg, milk, orange peel, juice, and cooking oil. Stir into dry ingredients till moistened. Stir in nuts. Drop by teaspoonfuls into deep hot fat (360°) and fry till brown, about 1½ minutes per side, turning once. Drain. Roll in sugar, if desired. Makes about 30 doughnuts.

Fritelle (Little Fried Cakes)

These Italian-style fried cakes make an excellent snack or sweet ending to a meal—

> 1 cup sifted cake flour
> 1¼ teaspoons baking powder
> ⅛ teaspoon salt
> 2 beaten egg yolks
> ¼ cup sugar
> ½ cup milk
> 2 egg whites
> Fat for frying
> Sugar

Sift together cake flour, baking powder, and salt. Beat egg yolks and ¼ cup sugar together till thick and lemon-colored. Add dry ingredients and milk alternately to egg mixture. Beat just till blended after each addition. Beat egg whites till stiff peaks form; fold into batter. Heat ½ inch cooking oil to 375° in skillet that is at least 2 inches deep. Drop batter by tablespoonfuls into hot fat. Fry till golden, about 1 minute per side, turning once. Drain on paper toweling. Sprinkle with sugar. Serve warm. Makes 16.

Rice Fritters

Try these for a nice change of pace from potatoes at your next Sunday dinner—

> 1 cup all-purpose flour
> 1½ teaspoons baking powder
> ¼ teaspoon salt
> 1 beaten egg
> 1 cup cooked rice
> ½ cup milk
> 3 tablespoons chopped green onion
>   with tops
> 2 tablespoons butter *or* margarine,
>   melted
> Fat for frying
> Grated Parmesan cheese

Thoroughly stir together the flour, baking powder, and salt. Combine egg, rice, milk, green onion, and butter or margarine. Add dry ingredients to egg mixture, stirring just till flour is moistened. Drop batter by rounded teaspoonfuls into deep hot fat (350°). Fry until golden brown, about 1½ minutes per side, turning once. Drain on paper toweling. Sprinkle with Parmesan cheese. Serve hot. Makes 32.

Jiffy Grape Bismarcks

Fry 1 package refrigerated biscuits in deep hot fat (375°) about 1 minute per side; turn once. Drain on paper toweling. When cool, make slit in side of each; fill with 1 teaspoon grape jelly. Roll in mixture of ¼ cup sugar and ¼ teaspoon ground cinnamon. Serve at once.

Corn Fritters

> 3 or 4 ears fresh corn*
> 1½ cups all-purpose flour
> 1 tablespoon baking powder
> 1 beaten egg
> 1 cup milk*
> Fat for frying

Cut kernels off ears of corn to make 1 cup. Stir together flour, baking powder, and ¾ teaspoon salt. Combine egg, milk, and corn. Stir into dry ingredients; mix just till moistened. Heat 1½ inches oil to 375° in skillet that is at least 3 inches deep. Drop batter by tablespoonfuls into hot fat. Fry until golden brown, 1½ to 2 minutes per side, turning once. Drain on paper toweling. Serve with warm maple syrup, if desired. Makes 24 fritters.

*Note: If desired, substitute one 8¾-ounce can whole kernel corn. Drain, reserving liquid; add milk to make 1 cup. Use to replace milk.

Drop fritter batter from a tablespoon into hot fat. Fry fritters on both sides until golden brown. Drain on paper toweling.

Pancakes and Waffles

When you want to make breakfast or brunch special, consider a pancake or waffle with all its variations. Or, if you are stumped for a dessert idea, try thin pancakes rolled around a fruit filling or waffles topped with ice cream or whipped cream and fruit.

To prepare the majority of pancake and waffle recipes, add the liquid ingredients (egg, milk, and oil) to the thoroughly stirred-together dry ingredients and beat only until the mixture is blended. The batter will be slightly lumpy, however, these lumps disappear during baking.

Follow the manufacturer's directions for using your waffle baker. However, when baking pancakes, test the temperature of the griddle or skillet by sprinkling with water. If drops of water dance across the surface, the heat is just right to start. During baking, if the pancakes appear to be baking too slowly, turn up the heat. If the cakes are baking too quickly, leaving uncooked centers, reduce the heat.

Keep pancakes hot for serving by piling them up on a paper-lined baking sheet and placing them in a warm oven. Put paper napkins or paper toweling between each layer to absorb the steam that makes them soggy. Keep waffles hot in the oven by putting them in a single layer on a rack placed on a baking sheet.

Blender Bread Crumb Pancakes

The blender turns leftover dry bread into a tasty breakfast treat—

> 2 slices dry bread
> 1½ cups buttermilk
> 2 eggs
> 2 tablespoons cooking oil
> 1½ cups all-purpose flour
> 1 teaspoon baking soda
> ½ teaspoon salt

Break dry bread slices into blender container; blend till in coarse dry crumbs. Add remaining ingredients to bread in blender container; blend just to combine. Drop batter by tablespoonfuls on hot, lightly greased griddle. Bake. (Small cakes are easier to manage.) Makes 24.

Feather Pancakes

> 1 cup all-purpose flour*
> 2 tablespoons sugar
> 2 tablespoons baking powder*
> ½ teaspoon salt*
> • • •
> 1 beaten egg
> 1 cup milk
> 2 tablespoons cooking oil

In mixing bowl thoroughly stir together the all-purpose flour, sugar, baking powder, and salt. Combine egg, milk, and cooking oil; add all at once to dry ingredients, beating till blended. Bake on hot, lightly greased griddle. Makes about 32 dollar-size pancakes or six to eight 4-inch pancakes.

*Note: When substituting self-rising all-purpose flour, omit the baking powder and salt.

Peanut Butter Pancakes: Prepare Feather Pancakes as above *except* beat egg with ⅓ cup chunk-style peanut butter till blended; reduce cooking oil to 1 tablespoon.

Pancake Mix Variety

Combine 2 cups complete pancake mix and 1⅓ cups water. Stir in 1 cup finely chopped fully cooked ham; *or* 1 cup fresh blueberries; *or* one 8-ounce can whole kernel corn, drained. Bake on hot, lightly greased griddle, using 2 tablespoons batter for each. Makes 18.

Low Fat Pancakes

In mixing bowl thoroughly stir together 1 cup all-purpose flour, 2 tablespoons sugar, 1 tablespoon baking powder, and ½ teaspoon salt. Combine 1 cup skim milk and 1 tablespoon cooking oil. Add to dry ingredients. Beat with rotary beater or electric mixer till smooth. Using clean beaters, beat 2 egg whites till stiff. Fold into batter. Bake on hot, lightly greased griddle. Makes eight 4-inch pancakes.

Use a measuring cup to pour the pancake batter onto a hot, lightly greased griddle. Use about ¼ cup batter for standard-size cakes and a tablespoonful for dollar-size cakes. Be sure to space the batter far enough apart so that the pancakes will not touch as they expand.

It's easy to tell when the pancakes are done on one side and should be turned. Two good indicators that the pancakes are ready to turn are a bubbly top with a few broken bubbles and slightly dry edges. Remember to turn the pancakes only once.

Hawaiian Hotcakes

Drizzle these Quick Bread Mix pancakes with a maple-flavored sausage-pineapple sauce—

    ½ pound bulk pork sausage
    4 teaspoons all-purpose flour
    ½ cup water
    1 8-ounce can crushed pineapple
        (juice pack)
    ½ cup maple-flavored syrup
            • • •
    1 beaten egg
    1⅓ cups milk
    2 cups Quick Bread Mix (see
        page 7)

Brown sausage in skillet, breaking up meat as it cooks. Drain well. Sprinkle meat with flour; mix well. Add water and cook, stirring constantly, till mixture thickens. Stir in undrained pineapple and maple-flavored syrup; simmer, covered, for 10 minutes. Combine egg and milk; add to Quick Bread Mix, beating till blended. Bake on hot, lightly greased griddle. Serve sauce over pancakes. Makes 16 pancakes and 2½ cups sauce.

Buttermilk Pancakes

Put lots of maple syrup and softened butter on the table when you serve these golden pancakes—

    1 cup all-purpose flour
    1 tablespoon sugar
    2 teaspoons baking powder
    ½ teaspoon baking soda
    ½ teaspoon salt
            • • •
    1 beaten egg
    1 cup buttermilk *or* sour milk*
    2 tablespoons cooking oil

In mixing bowl thoroughly stir together the all-purpose flour, sugar, baking powder, baking soda, and salt. In another bowl combine beaten egg, buttermilk or sour milk, and cooking oil; add to dry ingredients, beating till blended. Bake on hot, lightly greased griddle till golden. Makes eight 4-inch pancakes.

*Note: To make sour milk from fresh milk, place 1 tablespoon vinegar in measuring cup. Add enough fresh milk to make 1 cup liquid. Stir well and let mixture stand about 5 minutes before using in recipe.

Cottage Cheese-Filled Pancakes

    2 eggs
    1 cup light cream
    ½ cup all-purpose flour
    1½ teaspoons sugar
    ¼ teaspoon salt
        • • •
    1 cup cream-style cottage cheese
    1 tablespoon sugar
    ½ teaspoon vanilla
    Sunshine Sauce

Beat eggs just to blend; stir in cream. Add flour, 1½ teaspoons sugar, and salt; beat till smooth with rotary beater. Using 2 tablespoonfuls of batter for each pancake, spread batter for each on hot, lightly greased griddle to form a pancake 5 inches in diameter. Brown on both sides. Repeat to make 12 pancakes.

For filling, drain cottage cheese well; stir in 1 tablespoon sugar and vanilla. Divide between 12 pancakes; roll up. Place in 10x6x2-inch baking dish. Cover with foil. Bake at 350° till heated through, 15 to 20 minutes. Serve with Sunshine Sauce. Makes 6 servings.

Sunshine Sauce: In small saucepan melt 1 tablespoon butter *or* margarine; blend in 1 tablespoon cornstarch. Add 1 teaspoon grated orange peel, ⅔ cup orange juice, 2 tablespoons sugar, and dash salt. Cook and stir till thickened and bubbly. Blend in ½ cup light cream; heat through over low heat.

Oven Pancake

Cut sausages from one 8-ounce package brown-and-serve sausage links in half lengthwise. Brown the sausages in a skillet. Drain thoroughly and set aside. Thoroughly stir together 1 cup all-purpose flour, 2 tablespoons sugar, 1 tablespoon baking powder, and ½ teaspoon salt. Combine 1 beaten egg, ¾ cup milk, and 3 tablespoons butter *or* margarine, melted; add all at once to dry ingredients, beating till smooth. Turn batter into a greased and floured 15½x10½x1-inch baking pan, spreading the batter to edges of pan. Arrange the sausage halves, cut side down, atop batter in pan. Bake at 425° for 15 minutes. To serve, cut pancake into squares and pass maple syrup. Makes 6 servings.

Hashed Brown Potato Pancakes

    ½ of a 12-ounce package frozen
        fried hashed brown potatoes
        (1 cup)
    1 cup packaged pancake mix
    ¼ cup finely chopped onion
    ¼ teaspoon salt

Rinse and separate potatoes in hot water; drain well. Prepare pancake mix according to package directions. Stir in potatoes, onion, salt, and dash pepper. Bake on hot, lightly greased griddle, using ¼ cup batter for each pancake. Serve with maple syrup, if desired. Makes 12 to 14 pancakes.

Applesauce Flaps

    1½ cups all-purpose flour
    2 tablespoons sugar
    1 tablespoon baking powder
    ¼ teaspoon salt
    ⅛ teaspoon ground nutmeg
    2 beaten eggs
    1 cup milk
    1 cup applesauce
    2 tablespoons butter, melted
    Hot Apple Syrup

Stir together flour, sugar, baking powder, salt, and nutmeg. Combine eggs, milk, applesauce, and butter. Add to dry ingredients, beating till blended. Bake on hot, lightly greased griddle, using about 3 tablespoons batter for each pancake. Serve with Hot Apple Syrup. Makes 18 pancakes.

Hot Apple Syrup: In small saucepan heat together ½ cup apple jelly, 2 tablespoons butter *or* margarine, 2 tablespoons water, and ⅛ teaspoon ground cinnamon, stirring till melted and smooth. Makes about ½ cup syrup.

Deviled Ham Griddle Cakes

    1 cup packaged pancake mix
    1 3-ounce can deviled ham
    Maple syrup

Prepare pancake mix according to package directions; stir in deviled ham. Bake on hot, lightly greased griddle, turning once. Serve with maple syrup. Makes 8 pancakes.

Serve a stack of butter- and syrup-laden *Whole Wheat Pancakes* for enjoyable breakfast eating. The golden cakes are made with two kinds of flour and have their own special syrup. You will want to use the honey- and maple-flavored syrup for other breakfast specials.

Whole Wheat Pancakes

　1¼ cups whole wheat flour
　　¾ cup all-purpose flour
　　2 tablespoons packed brown sugar
　　1 tablespoon baking powder
　　½ teaspoon salt
　　　　• • •
　　2 beaten eggs
　1½ cups milk
　　3 tablespoons cooking oil *or* melted
　　　　shortening
　　　Honey Syrup

Thoroughly stir together the whole wheat flour, all-purpose flour, brown sugar, baking powder, and salt. Beat together eggs, milk, and oil or melted shortening; add to dry ingredients, beating till blended. Bake on hot, lightly greased griddle, using 2 tablespoons batter for each pancake. Serve with Honey Syrup. Makes 24 pancakes.

　Honey Syrup: Heat together ⅔ cup honey and ⅓ cup maple-flavored syrup.

Vita Pancakes

　　1 cup all-purpose flour
　　¼ cup whole bran cereal
　　2 tablespoons wheat germ
　　2 teaspoons baking powder
　　1 teaspoon sugar
　　¼ teaspoon salt
　　1 egg yolk
　　1 cup orange juice
　　2 tablespoons cooking oil
　　1 stiffly beaten egg white
　　　Orange Syrup

Thoroughly stir together the all-purpose flour, whole bran cereal, wheat germ, baking powder, sugar, and salt. Beat together the egg yolk, orange juice, and cooking oil till thick; add to dry ingredients, beating till blended. Fold in egg white. Bake on hot, lightly greased griddle, turning once. Serve with Orange Syrup. Makes eight 4-inch pancakes.

　Orange Syrup: Blend together ⅔ cup orange marmalade and ⅓ cup maple-flavored syrup.

To prepare waffle batter, stir together the dry ingredients. Combine the liquid ingredients and add to the dry mixture, beating just till blended. (Batter will be slightly lumpy.) Some waffle recipes specify folding stiffly beaten egg whites into the batter. Avoid overmixing by allowing small fluffs of beaten egg white to remain interspersed throughout batter.

Pour the waffle batter onto grids of a preheated waffle baker. Close lid quickly; do not open during baking. Waffles are done when the steam stops escaping from sides of waffle baker or when the indicator light signals. For crisp waffles, allow the waffle to remain on grid a few seconds after opening lid. Or, bake waffles a little longer for extra crispness.

Everyday Waffles

Versatile waffles are equally as good served with whipped cream and fresh fruit as they are with butter and your favorite syrup—

  1¾ **cups all-purpose flour**
    1 **tablespoon baking powder**
    ½ **teaspoon salt**
      • • •
    2 **beaten egg yolks**
  1¾ **cups milk**
    ½ **cup cooking oil** *or* **melted**
       shortening
      • • •
    2 **stiffly beaten egg whites**

In mixing bowl thoroughly stir together the flour, baking powder, and salt. Combine egg yolks, milk, and cooking oil or melted shortening; add to dry ingredients, beating just till blended. Carefully fold in stiffly beaten egg whites, leaving a few fluffs of egg white— *do not overmix.* Bake in preheated waffle baker. Makes three 9-inch waffles.

Pumpkin-Nut Waffles

    2 **cups all-purpose flour**
    1 **tablespoon baking powder**
    ¾ **teaspoon pumpkin pie spice**
    ¼ **teaspoon salt**
    3 **egg yolks**
  1¾ **cups milk**
    ½ **cup cooking oil** *or* **melted**
       shortening
    ½ **cup canned pumpkin**
    3 **stiffly beaten egg whites**
    ½ **cup chopped walnuts**

In mxing bowl thoroughly stir together the flour, baking powder, pumpkin pie spice, and salt. Beat egg yolks till thick and lemon-colored; stir in milk, oil, and pumpkin. Add to dry ingredients, beating just till blended. Carefully fold in stiffly beaten egg whites, leaving a few fluffs of egg white. Stir in chopped walnuts. Bake in preheated waffle baker. Serve hot waffles with maple syrup, if desired. Makes five 9-inch waffles.

Apricot-Sauced Pecan Waffles

See these golden-sauced waffles on pages 60 and 61 —

  2¼ cups all-purpose flour
  4 teaspoons baking powder
  1½ tablespoons sugar
  ¾ teaspoon salt
  ½ teaspoon grated orange peel
  2 beaten eggs
  2¼ cups milk
  ½ cup cooking oil
  1 cup chopped pecans
    Apricot Sauce

In mixing bowl thoroughly stir together the flour, baking powder, sugar, salt, and grated orange peel. Combine eggs, milk, and cooking oil; add all at once to dry ingredients, beating just till blended. Spread batter in preheated waffle baker; sprinkle with *one-third* of the pecans. Bake. Repeat. Serve with Apricot Sauce. Makes three 9-inch waffles.

Apricot Sauce: Drain one 8¾-ounce can unpeeled apricot halves, reserving the syrup. Chop fruit; set aside. In saucepan blend reserved syrup, ½ cup maple-flavored syrup, 2 tablespoons cornstarch, 2 tablespoons honey, 1 tablespoon lemon juice, and dash salt. Stir in 1 cup apricot nectar. Cook and stir over medium heat till mixture thickens and bubbles. Stir in apricots; heat through. Makes 2½ cups.

Chocolate Waffles

Try these for an unusual dessert —

  1 beaten egg
  ¾ cup milk
  ¼ cup chocolate-flavored syrup
  2 tablespoons cooking oil
  1 cup packaged buttermilk
    pancake mix
  ⅓ cup chopped pecans
  ¼ cup butter *or* margarine
  ¼ cup sifted powdered sugar
  1 tablespoon unsweetened cocoa
    powder

Beat together egg, milk, syrup, and oil. Add to pancake mix, beating just till blended. Stir in nuts. Bake in preheated waffle baker till done. Meanwhile, cream together butter, sugar, and cocoa powder till fluffy. Serve with hot waffles. Makes two 9-inch waffles.

Quick Bread Mix Waffles

  2 beaten egg yolks
  1⅓ cups milk
  2 tablespoons cooking oil
  2 cups Quick Bread Mix (see
    page 7)
  2 stiffly beaten egg whites

In bowl combine egg yolks, milk, and cooking oil. Add to Quick Bread Mix, beating just till blended. Carefully fold in stiffly beaten egg whites, leaving a few fluffs of egg white — *do not overmix.* Bake in preheated waffle baker. Makes three 9-inch waffles.

Banana Waffles: Prepare Quick Bread Mix Waffles as above *except* stir 1 medium banana, mashed (1 cup), and 2 tablespoons sugar into Quick Bread Mix along with liquid ingredients. Beat just till blended. Fold in egg whites. Bake. Makes three 9-inch waffles.

Berry-Topped Banana Waffles

    Banana Waffles (above)
  1 pint vanilla ice cream,
    softened
  1 8-ounce carton strawberry
    yogurt
  1 10-ounce package frozen straw-
    berries, thawed, *or* 1 pint
    fresh strawberries, sliced

Prepare Banana Waffles. Meanwhile, combine softened ice cream and yogurt. For each serving, spoon ice cream mixture between two waffle squares and add a dollop on top. Drizzle with strawberries. Makes 6 servings.

Peanut Butter Waffles

  1 cup packaged pancake mix
  2 tablespoons sugar
  ⅓ cup chunk-style peanut butter
  1 beaten egg
  1 cup milk
  2 tablespoons cooking oil

Combine pancake mix and sugar. Mix peanut butter, egg, milk, and oil; add to dry ingredients. Beat just till blended. Bake in preheated waffle baker. Makes two 9-inch waffles.

Cornmeal Specialties

Wheat Germ Corn Bread

This nutritious corn bread is seen on page 4 —

  1 cup all-purpose flour
  1 cup yellow *or* white cornmeal
  ¾ cup wheat germ
  ⅓ cup sugar
  5 teaspoons baking powder
  2 beaten eggs
  1½ cups milk
  ⅓ cup cooking oil

Stir together the first 5 ingredients and 1 teaspoon salt. Combine eggs, milk, and oil; add to dry ingredients, stirring till blended. Turn into greased 9x9x2-inch baking pan. Bake at 425° for 25 to 30 minutes. Serves 9.

Southern Corn Bread

  2 cups white cornmeal
  1 tablespoon baking powder
  ½ teaspoon baking soda
  2 eggs
  1 cup buttermilk
  ¼ cup lard, melted

Stir together cornmeal, baking powder, baking soda, and ¾ teaspoon salt. Add eggs, buttermilk, and melted lard. Beat with electric mixer or rotary beater just till smooth, about 1 minute. Turn into greased 10-inch oven-going skillet. Bake at 425° for 20 to 25 minutes. Serve with butter, if desired. Makes 6 servings.

Perfect Corn Bread

Stir together 1 cup all-purpose flour, 1 cup yellow cornmeal, ¼ cup sugar, 4 teaspoons baking powder, and ¾ teaspoon salt. Add 2 beaten eggs, 1 cup milk, and ¼ cup shortening. Beat with rotary beater just till smooth. (Do not overbeat.) Turn into greased 9x9x2-inch baking pan. Bake at 425° for 20 to 25 minutes. Serves 9.

  Corn Sticks: Spoon batter into greased corn stick pans, filling pans ⅔ full. Bake at 425° for 12 to 15 minutes. Makes 18.

Buttermilk Corn Bread

  1 cup all-purpose flour
  1 cup yellow cornmeal
  2 teaspoons baking powder
  ¾ teaspoon salt
  ½ teaspoon baking soda
  2 beaten egg yolks
  1 cup buttermilk
  3 tablespoons butter *or* margarine, melted
  2 stiffly beaten egg whites

In a mixing bowl thoroughly stir together the all-purpose flour, cornmeal, baking powder, salt, and baking soda. Combine egg yolks, buttermilk, and melted butter or margarine; add to dry ingredients, beating till blended. Fold in stiffly beaten egg whites. Turn batter into greased 8x8x2-inch baking pan. Bake at 350° for 25 to 30 minutes. Makes 8 servings.

Two-Corn Bread

This moist corn bread is made with both cornmeal and cream-style corn —

  1 cup all-purpose flour
  1 cup yellow cornmeal
  2 tablespoons sugar
  1 tablespoon baking powder
  ¼ teaspoon salt
  3 eggs
  1 cup cream-style cottage cheese
  1 8-ounce can cream-style corn

Stir together flour, cornmeal, sugar, baking powder, and salt. Beat eggs and cottage cheese till smooth; stir in corn. Add to dry ingredients; stir just till blended. Turn into greased 9x9x2-inch baking pan. Bake at 375° for 30 to 35 minutes. Serve warm. Makes 9 servings.

Who could resist big squares of warm, freshly-cut *Buttermilk Corn Bread?* Spread with softened butter and drizzled with sweet honey, the tender squares make the perfect mate to your special chicken dinner or outdoor barbecue.

Cheesy Spoon Bread

Eat this puffy, souffle-like spoon bread from dishes. It's pictured on pages 60 and 61—

> 1 cup yellow cornmeal
> 1½ cups water
> • • •
> 1 cup milk
> ½ cup grated Parmesan cheese
>   (2 ounces)
> 2 tablespoons butter *or* margarine,
>   melted
> 2 teaspoons sugar
> 2 teaspoons baking powder
> ½ teaspoon salt
> 3 beaten egg yolks
> 3 stiffly beaten egg whites
>   Butter *or* margarine

In saucepan combine cornmeal and water. Cook, stirring constantly, till mixture is the consistency of mush. Remove from heat; stir in milk, cheese, 2 tablespoons butter, sugar, baking powder, and salt. Stir in egg yolks; carefully fold in egg whites. (Batter will be thin.) Bake in greased 1½-quart casserole at 325° for 55 to 60 minutes. Serve immediately with butter. Makes 6 to 8 servings.

Farina Corn Bread

Try this corn bread in a convenient loaf which slices nicely after cooling—

> ¾ cup all-purpose flour
> ¾ cup yellow cornmeal
> ¼ cup quick-cooking farina
> 3 tablespoons sugar
> 2 teaspoons baking powder
> ½ teaspoon baking soda
> ½ teaspoon salt
> 1 beaten egg
> ⅔ cup milk
> 3 tablespoons cooking oil *or*
>   melted shortening

In mixing bowl thoroughly stir together the flour, cornmeal, farina, sugar, baking powder, baking soda, and salt. Combine egg, milk, and cooking oil; add all at once to dry ingredients, stirring just till dry ingredients are moistened. Bake in greased 8½x4½x2½-inch loaf pan at 375° about 25 minutes. Remove loaf from pan; cool on wire rack. Makes 1 loaf.

Tomato-Corn Spoon Bread

> ¾ cup yellow cornmeal
> 1 cup milk
> 1 8-ounce can whole kernel corn,
>   drained and slightly mashed
> 1 8-ounce can tomatoes, undrained,
>   *or* 2 chopped, peeled tomatoes
>   (1 cup)
> ¼ cup butter *or* margarine,
>   softened
> 2 teaspoons sugar
> 2 teaspoons baking powder
> 1 teaspoon salt
> 4 beaten egg yolks
> 4 stiffly beaten egg whites
> 2 tablespoons grated Parmesan
>   cheese

In saucepan combine cornmeal and milk. Cook, stirring constantly, till mixture is the consistency of mush. Remove from heat; stir in corn, tomatoes, butter, sugar, baking powder, and salt. Stir in egg yolks. Carefully fold in egg whites. Pour mixture into greased 8x8-x2-inch baking dish. Sprinkle with Parmesan cheese. Bake at 375° till center is firm, 20 to 25 minutes. Serve hot. Makes 6 servings.

Cheesy Corn Muffins

Attractive, cheesy muffins with poppy seed topping that make an excellent accompaniment to a salad—

> 1 cup all-purpose flour
> ¾ cup yellow cornmeal
> 2 tablespoons sugar
> 1 tablespoon baking powder
> ½ teaspoon salt
> 1 beaten egg
> 1 cup milk
> 1 cup shredded sharp American cheese
>   (4 ounces)
> ¼ cup cooking oil *or* melted
>   shortening
>   Poppy seed

In mixing bowl stir together the flour, cornmeal, sugar, baking powder, and salt. Combine egg, milk, cheese, and cooking oil; add to dry ingredients, stirring just till cornmeal mixture is moistened. Fill well-greased muffin pans ⅔ full. Sprinkle with poppy seed. Bake at 400° for 20 to 25 minutes. Makes 12 muffins.

Fill a napkin-lined basket with warm, golden *Sour Cream-Corn Muffins* and watch this tasty quick bread disappear before a happy family or friends. Be sure to have lots of butter on the table for spreading. You're sure to be asked to make more of these muffins soon.

Sour Cream-Corn Muffins

These taste like miniature corn breads—

1⅓ cups yellow cornmeal
⅓ cup all-purpose flour
2 tablespoons packed brown sugar
1 teaspoon baking powder
½ teaspoon baking soda
½ teaspoon salt
• • •
1 beaten egg
1 cup dairy sour cream
⅓ cup milk
2 tablespoons cooking oil

In mixing bowl thoroughly stir together the cornmeal, flour, sugar, baking powder, baking soda, and salt; make a well in center. Combine egg, sour cream, milk, and cooking oil; add all at once to dry ingredients, stirring just till dry ingredients are moistened. Fill greased muffin pans or paper bake cup-lined muffin pans ⅔ full. Bake at 400° for 20 to 25 minutes. Serve warm. Makes 12 muffins.

Cornmeal-Pumpkin Muffins

Sweet pumpkin and spice give these muffins their interesting flavor—

1½ cups all-purpose flour
½ cup yellow cornmeal
1 tablespoon baking powder
1 teaspoon salt
½ teaspoon ground cinnamon
½ teaspoon ground nutmeg
• • •
1 beaten egg
½ cup canned pumpkin
½ cup milk
¼ cup honey
¼ cup cooking oil

In mixing bowl thoroughly stir together flour, cornmeal, baking powder, salt, cinnamon, and nutmeg. Combine egg, pumpkin, milk, honey, and oil; add all at once to dry ingredients, sitrring just till dry ingredients are moistened. Fill greased muffin pans ⅔ full. Bake at 400° for 20 to 25 minutes. Makes 12 muffins.

Hush Puppies

Especially popular in the South —

   2 cups chopped onion
   ⅓ cup water
   1½ cups white cornmeal
   ½ cup all-purpose flour
   1½ teaspoons baking powder
   1¼ teaspoons salt
   1 cup cold water
   ¼ cup butter *or* margarine
   White cornmeal
   Shortening for frying

In medium saucepan cook onion, covered, in ⅓ cup water for 2 to 3 minutes. Thoroughly stir together 1½ cups cornmeal, flour, baking powder, and salt; stir in the 1 cup cold water. Gradually spoon cornmeal dough into onions. Remove from heat; add butter or margarine, stirring to melt butter.

   Fill pie plate with cornmeal. Drop 2 to 3 tablespoons of the dough for each hush puppy into the cornmeal. Roll in cornmeal and form into oblong shape. Fry in 2 to 3 inches hot fat (365°) till done, about 3 minutes. Drain on paper toweling. Keep warm. Makes 16.

To make *Potato-Corn Triangles*, knead and roll dough on well-floured surface to 9-inch circle. Cut into 12 even triangles with sharp knife.

Corn Bread Cakes

   1 8- or 14-ounce package corn
   muffin mix
   2 tablespoons nonfat dry milk
   powder
   1 egg

Combine muffin mix and milk powder. Beat egg and ⅓ cup water till blended; add to mix, stirring just till moistened. Drop in mounds on lightly greased griddle or skillet, using about 2 tablespoons for each. Cook over low heat, turning to brown both sides, about 6 minutes. Serve with butter, if desired. Makes 8.

Johnnycakes

   2 cups yellow *or* white cornmeal
   1½ cups milk
   1 beaten egg
   1 tablespoon cooking oil

Combine cornmeal, milk, egg, cooking oil, and 1 teaspoon salt; mix well. For each, drop a scant ¼ cup batter onto a well-greased hot griddle, spreading about ¼ inch thick. Cook over medium heat to a golden brown, 2 to 3 minutes on each side. Serve warm with butter and syrup, if desired. Makes 10 johnnycakes.

Potato-Corn Triangles

These golden wedges are seen on page 25 —

   ⅔ cup packaged instant mashed
   potato flakes
   ⅓ cup shortening
   1¼ cups all-purpose flour
   ½ cup yellow cornmeal
   4 teaspoons baking powder
   ½ teaspoon salt
   ½ cup milk

Combine instant potato flakes and ⅔ cup hot water; stir till water is absorbed. Blend in shortening. Stir together flour, cornmeal, baking powder, and salt; add to potato mixture. Stir in milk till dry ingredients are moistened. Knead gently on well-floured surface (3 or 4 strokes). Roll dough to 9-inch circle. Cut into 12 triangles. Place on ungreased baking sheet 2 inches apart. Bake at 400° for 20 to 25 minutes. Makes 12 triangles.

Cornmeal Pie

Pie-shaped wedges are a great base for your favorite meat sauces or they are delicious simply served with butter—

    ⅔ cup yellow cornmeal
    2 cups milk
        • • •
    1 cup shredded American cheese
        (4 ounces)
    1 tablespoon butter *or* margarine
    ¾ teaspoon baking powder
    ½ teaspoon salt
    ¼ teaspoon paprika
    2 slightly beaten egg yolks
    2 stiffly beaten egg whites

In medium saucepan cook cornmeal and milk, stirring constantly, till mixture is the consistency of mush. Add cheese, butter or margarine, baking powder, salt, and paprika; stir till cheese melts and ingredients are blended. Gradually add a little hot mixture to egg yolks; beat well and return to hot mixture. Carefully fold in egg whites. Turn into greased 9-inch pie plate. Bake at 350° for 40 to 45 minutes. Makes 6 servings.

Corn Bread Coffee Cake

Change the flavor of the preserves each time you make this unusual coffee cake—

    1 cup all-purpose flour
    1 cup yellow cornmeal
    2 tablespoons sugar
    1 tablespoon baking powder
    ½ teaspoon salt
        • • •
    1 beaten egg
    1 cup milk
    3 tablespoons cooking oil
    ½ cup strawberry preserves
    1 tablespoon sugar

In mixing bowl thoroughly stir together the flour, cornmeal, 2 tablespoons sugar, baking powder, and salt. Combine egg, milk, and cooking oil; add to dry ingredients, stirring just till dry ingredients are blended. Spread batter evenly in greased 9-inch pie plate; spoon strawberry preserves over batter. Sprinkle top with the remaining 1 tablespoon sugar. Bake at 425° for 20 to 25 minutes. Serves 6 to 8.

Cornmeal Pancakes

    1½ cups all-purpose flour
    ½ cup yellow cornmeal
    2 tablespoons sugar
    1 teaspoon baking soda
    1 teaspoon salt
    2 beaten eggs
    2 cups buttermilk
    2 tablespoons butter, melted

In mixing bowl thoroughly stir together the flour, cornmeal, sugar, baking soda, and salt. Combine the eggs, buttermilk, and melted butter; add to dry ingredients, beating till blended. Bake on hot, lightly greased griddle, using ¼ cup batter for each pancake. Makes sixteen 4-inch pancakes.

Cornmeal Waffles

    1 cup all-purpose flour
    1 cup yellow cornmeal
    2 teaspoons baking powder
    1 teaspoon baking soda
    1 teaspoon sugar
    2 beaten egg yolks
    2 cups buttermilk
    ¼ cup cooking oil
    2 stiffly beaten egg whites

In mixing bowl thoroughly stir together the flour, cornmeal, baking powder, baking soda, sugar, and ½ teaspoon salt. Combine egg yolks, buttermilk, and cooking oil; add to dry ingredients, beating just till blended. Carefully fold in stiffly beaten egg whites, leaving a few fluffs of egg white. Bake in preheated waffle baker. Makes three 9-inch waffles.

Fried Cornmeal Mush

Combine 1 cup yellow cornmeal, 1 cup cold water, 1 teaspoon salt, and 1 teaspoon sugar; gradually add to 2¾ cups boiling water, stirring constantly. Cook till thick, stirring frequently. Cover; cook over low heat for 10 to 15 minutes. Pour into 7½x3½x2-inch loaf pan. Cool; chill several hours or overnight. Turn out; cut in ½-inch thick slices. Fry slowly in hot fat; turn once. When browned, serve with butter and syrup. Makes 6 servings.

Convenience Bread Dress-Ups

Orange Coffee Ring

1 loaf frozen white bread dough
  (1 pound)
3 tablespoons butter *or* margarine
½ cup orange marmalade
⅓ cup chopped almonds, toasted
2 tablespoons butter *or* margarine,
  melted
⅓ cup sugar
½ teaspoon ground cinnamon

Thaw frozen dough for 1½ to 2 hours at room temperature. With knife, cut dough into 6 slices. Cut each into thirds, making 18 pieces.

In small saucepan melt 3 tablespoons butter. Stir in orange marmalade and nuts. Form each piece of dough into a small ball. Roll in the remaining 2 tablespoons melted butter, then in a mixture of the sugar and cinnamon. Place *half* the balls in well-greased 9-inch tube pan. Spoon *half* the marmalade mixture atop. Repeat with remaining balls and marmalade mixture. Cover and let rise in warm place till almost double, about 2 hours. Bake at 375° for 30 minutes. Invert at once onto plate.

Cherry Filled Rolls

1 loaf frozen white bread dough
  (1 pound)
1½ cups canned cherry pie filling
1 cup sifted powdered sugar
1 to 2 tablespoons milk

Thaw frozen dough for 1½ to 2 hours at room temperature. Roll out on lightly floured surface to 18x10-inch rectangle. Cut in eighteen 10-inch strips. Roll each strip into a rope. Coil ropes loosely to form round rolls. Place on greased baking sheet. Gently press center of each roll and fill each with about 2 teaspoons of the cherry filling. Cover and let rise in warm place till almost double, about 1 hour. Bake at 375° for 15 to 20 minutes. Combine powdered sugar and enough milk to make of drizzling consistency. Drizzle over warm rolls. Makes 18 rolls.

Butterscotch Rolls

1 loaf frozen white bread dough
1 3¾- or 4-ounce package *regular*
  butterscotch pudding mix
½ cup chopped walnuts
¼ cup packed brown sugar
2 tablespoons butter, melted
1 teaspoon vanilla
½ teaspoon ground cinnamon

Thaw frozen dough for 1½ to 2 hours at room temperature or overnight in refrigerator. With sharp knife or scissors, cut crosswise into twelve ½-inch slices. Combine remaining ingredients. Cover bottom of greased 9-inch fluted or regular tube pan with *half* of the slices of dough; sprinkle with *half* of the butterscotch mixture. Repeat layers. Cover and let rise till almost double, about 2 hours. Bake at 350° for 30 to 35 minutes. Immediately invert onto serving plate. Serve warm.

Herb Loaf Italiano

1 loaf frozen white bread dough
¼ cup butter *or* margarine,
  softened
2 tablespoons spaghetti sauce mix
2 tablespoons snipped parsley

Thaw frozen dough for 1½ to 2 hours at room temperature. Roll out to 12x9-inch rectangle. Combine butter, spaghetti sauce mix, and parsley; spread on dough. Roll up jelly-roll fashion starting with long side; seal seam. Place on greased baking sheet, seam side down. Brush with water; sprinkle with a little salt. Cover and let rise till almost double, about 2 hours. Make shallow slashes across top at 2-inch intervals. Bake at 375° about 30 minutes.

No one will know you didn't spend hours in the kitchen to make mouth-watering *Orange Coffee Ring* or *Cherry Filled Rolls*. Convenient frozen bread dough allows you to enjoy these homemade treats without all the fuss.

Creamy Cinnamon Rolls

Pour whipping cream over cinnamon roll slices before baking—

- **1 loaf frozen white bread dough (1 pound)**
- **2 tablespoons butter, melted**
- **⅔ cup packed brown sugar**
- **½ cup chopped walnuts**
- **1 teaspoon ground cinnamon**
- **½ cup whipping cream**
- **⅔ cup sifted powdered sugar**
- **1 tablespoon milk**

Thaw frozen dough for 1½ to 2 hours at room temperature. Roll dough to 18x6-inch rectangle. Brush with melted butter. Combine brown sugar, nuts, and cinnamon; sprinkle evenly over dough. Roll up jelly-roll fashion starting with long side; seal seam. Cut into 20 slices. Place rolls, cut side down, in two 8x1½-inch round baking pans. Cover and let rise till almost double, about 1½ hours. Pour cream over rolls. Bake at 350° for 25 minutes. While warm, drizzle with mixture of powdered sugar and milk. Makes 20.

Apricot-Date Coffee Cake

The recipe bonus is two delicious coffee treats from one single recipe—

- **1 loaf frozen white bread dough (1 pound)**
- **¼ cup apricot preserves**
- **¼ cup snipped pitted dates**
- **Confectioners' Icing (see page 13)**

Thaw frozen dough for 1½ to 2 hours at room temperature. Divide dough in half. On floured surface, roll one half into 12x7-inch rectangle. Cut up large pieces of apricot in preserves; spread *half* the preserves down center third of dough; sprinkle with *half* the dates. Fold long sides over to meet at center of filling; seal seam. Place on greased baking sheet, seam side down.

Snip strips every 1 inch almost to center of coffee cake down long sides. Turn each strip so cut side is up. Repeat with remaining dough and filling, making a second coffee cake. Cover and let rise till almost double, about 1 hour. Bake at 350° for 20 minutes. Drizzle tops with Confectioners' Icing. Makes 2 coffee cakes.

Shortcut Pecan Rolls

- **1 loaf frozen white bread dough**
- **¼ cup butter *or* margarine**
- **½ cup packed brown sugar**
- **1 tablespoon light corn syrup**
- **½ cup chopped pecans**
- **2 tablespoons butter, melted**
- **1 tablespoon granulated sugar**
- **½ teaspoon ground cinnamon**

Thaw frozen dough for 1½ to 2 hours at room temperature. With knife, cut into 6 slices. Cut each slice into thirds, making 18 pieces. Melt ¼ cup butter; remove from heat and stir in brown sugar and corn syrup. Divide mixture among 18 well-greased muffin cups; sprinkle with pecans. Place a piece of dough in each. Brush rolls with 2 tablespoons melted butter. Combine granulated sugar and cinnamon; sprinkle atop dough. Cover and let rise till almost double, about 1 hour. Bake at 375° for 15 to 20 minutes. Invert on rack. Makes 18.

Homemade Sandwich Buns

Thaw 1 loaf frozen white bread dough. Divide into 8 portions. Shape each into flattened round bun, rolling lightly with rolling pin to about a 3-inch diameter. Place on baking sheet. Cover and let rise till double, about 1 hour. Brush tops with water; sprinkle with poppy seed. Bake at 350° for 20 minutes. Makes 8.

Shortcut Beer Bread

- **¾ cup dark *or* light beer**
- **2 tablespoons butter *or* margarine**
- **1 13¾-ounce package hot roll mix**
- **1 egg**
- **2 tablespoons sugar**
- **½ cup wheat germ**

In saucepan heat beer and butter just till warm. Pour into mixing bowl; add yeast from hot roll mix and dissolve. Add egg, sugar, wheat germ, and dry ingredients of roll mix; mix well. Place in greased bowl. Cover and let rise till double, 45 to 60 minutes. Punch down; knead and shape into loaf. Place in greased 8½x4½x2½-inch loaf pan. Let rise 35 minutes. Bake at 350° for 40 to 45 minutes.

Biscuit Waffles

Separate rolls from 1 package refrigerated butterflake rolls (12 rolls). While still cold, separate each roll into 2 layers. For each waffle, arrange 4 layers, sides just touching, in preheated waffle baker. Bake till golden, about 2 minutes. Makes six 4-inch waffles.

Bacon Biscuit Waffles: Separate rolls from package as above *except* separate each roll into 4 layers. For each waffle, place a small amount of finely crumbled, cooked bacon atop one layer, cover with another layer, and arrange 4 filled biscuits, sides just touching, in preheated waffle baker. Bake about 2 minutes. Serve hot with butter and syrup.

Brunch Cakes

    1 3-ounce package cream cheese,
        softened
    2 tablespoons sugar
    1 egg yolk
    ¼ teaspoon vanilla
    ¼ cup crushed pineapple, drained
    1 package refrigerated butterflake
        rolls (12 rolls)

Beat together cheese, sugar, egg yolk, and vanilla; stir in pineapple. Flatten each biscuit on ungreased baking sheet to a 2½-inch circle, building up rim on sides. Spoon about *1 tablespoon* filling in center of each. Bake at 375° for 10 to 12 minutes. Serve warm. Makes 12.

Instant French Bread

    1 package refrigerated biscuits
        (10 biscuits)
    1 slightly beaten egg white
    1 tablespoon sesame seed, toasted

For 2 small loaves: Separate biscuits. Place 5 biscuits with sides touching, in a long row on greased baking sheet, forming a loaf. Press biscuits together slightly. Repeat with remaining biscuits. *For 1 double loaf:* Make 2 long loaves as above and press the loaves together side by side on greased baking sheet. Brush top with egg white; sprinkle with sesame seed. Bake at 350° about 20 minutes. Serve warm. Makes 2 small or 1 double loaf.

Quick Mincemeat Rolls

    ¼ cup caramel topping
    ¼ cup prepared mincemeat
    1 package refrigerated biscuits
        (10 biscuits)

Stir together caramel topping and mincemeat; spread mixture in bottom of greased 8x1½-inch round baking pan. Separate biscuits; place biscuits over mixture in pan. Bake at 400° for 15 to 20 minutes. Cool 1 minute. Invert rolls on plate; serve immediately.

Layered Parmesan Loaf

    1 package refrigerated biscuits
        (10 biscuits)
    2 tablespoons butter *or* margarine,
        melted
    ¼ cup grated Parmesan cheese

Separate biscuits; dip tops in melted butter, then in cheese. Arrange, cheese side up, overlapping in 2 rows on baking sheet. Bake at 450° about 12 minutes. Serve warm. Makes 10.

To make *Layered Parmesan Loaf*, arrange in two rows on baking sheet refrigerated biscuits, dipped in melted butter and cheese.

Orange Coffee Cake

Turn this sweet coffee treat out of the baking pan onto your prettiest serving plate—

2 tablespoons butter *or* margarine
⅓ cup sugar
1 tablespoon frozen orange juice
     concentrate, thawed
¼ teaspoon ground cinnamon
¼ cup chopped pecans
1 package refrigerated biscuits
     (10 biscuits)

Melt butter in 8x1½-inch round baking pan. Stir in sugar, orange juice concentrate, and cinnamon. Sprinkle with pecans. Separate biscuits; arrange biscuits atop nuts. Bake at 350° for 20 to 25 minutes. Cool 1 minute. Invert onto serving plate; serve warm. Serves 8.

Lemon Tea Rolls

Lemon flavor comes from a package of lemon-flavored gelatin; almonds complement flavor—

½ of a 3-ounce package lemon-
     flavored gelatin
     (3 tablespoons)
2 tablespoons sugar
1 package refrigerated biscuits
     (10 biscuits)
2 tablespoons butter, melted
¼ cup sliced almonds

Combine gelatin and sugar. Separate biscuits; dip tops in butter, then in lemon-sugar mixture. Arrange, sugared side up, in well-greased 8x1½-inch round baking pan. Sprinkle with nuts. Bake at 425° about 15 minutes. Serve warm. Makes 10.

Orange Rum Buns

1 package refrigerated biscuits
     (10 biscuits)
10 sugar cubes
¼ cup rum
2 teaspoons grated orange peel

Separate biscuits; place in greased muffin pans. Dip each sugar cube in rum just long enough to absorb some moisture; press sugar into center of each biscuit. Sprinkle tops with peel. Bake at 400° about 10 minutes. Makes 10.

To make *Sesame Biscuits*, place biscuits on ungreased baking sheet. Brush with a little milk, and sprinkle with toasted sesame seed.

Sesame Biscuits

1 package refrigerated biscuits
     (10 biscuits)
  Milk
1 tablespoon sesame seed,
     toasted

Separate biscuits; place on ungreased baking sheet. Brush tops with milk. Sprinkle with sesame seed. Bake at 400° about 10 minutes. Makes 10.

Crunchy Biscuit Ring

1¼ cups crisp rice cereal,
     slightly crushed
½ teaspoon salt
½ teaspoon dried dillweed
1 package refrigerated biscuits
     (10 biscuits)
2 to 3 tablespoons milk

Combine rice cereal, salt, and dillweed. Separate biscuits; dip in milk, then in cereal mixture. Arrange biscuits in ring, overlapping slightly, on greased baking sheet. Bake at 425° about 15 minutes. Loosen and slide onto serving plate. Serve warm. Makes 10.

Easy-Do Bacon Roll-Ups

These are perfect served at brunch with a big, cheese omelet or a bowl of hearty soup—

- **1 package refrigerated crescent rolls (8 rolls)**
- **6 slices bacon, crisp-cooked, drained, and crumbled**
- **2 tablespoons snipped green onion *or* chives**

Unroll crescent rolls and separate. Sprinkle each with bacon and green onion. Roll up dough, starting with wide end. Place on ungreased baking sheet, point side down. Bake at 375° for 12 to 15 minutes. Makes 8 rolls.

Thyme-Buttered Crescents

Lemon juice adds a little tang to the herb butter—

- **¼ cup butter *or* margarine, softened**
- **1 teaspoon lemon juice**
- **¼ teaspoon dried thyme, crushed**
- **1 package refrigerated crescent rolls (8 rolls)**

Cream butter or margarine till fluffy. Stir in lemon juice and thyme. Keep herb butter at room temperature for 1 hour to mellow before using. Unroll crescent rolls and separate; spread each with herb butter. Roll up dough, starting with wide end. Place on ungreased baking sheet, point side down. Bake at 350° about 15 minutes. Makes 8 rolls.

Onion Rolls

Fresh parsley and grated cheese add flavor—

- **½ cup finely chopped onion**
- **1 tablespoon butter *or* margarine**
- **1 tablespoon snipped parsley**
- **1 package refrigerated crescent rolls (8 rolls)**
- **Grated Parmesan cheese**

Cook onion in butter till tender but not brown. Stir in parsley. Unroll crescent rolls and separate; spread each with onion butter. Sprinkle generously with grated cheese; roll up dough, starting with wide end. Place on ungreased baking sheet, point side down. Bake at 400° for 8 to 10 minutes. Makes 8 rolls.

Poppy Seed Crescent Loaf

See this attractive loaf on pages 60 and 61—

- **¼ cup poppy seed**
- **¼ cup chopped nuts**
- **2 tablespoons honey**
- **½ teaspoon grated lemon peel**
- **1 stiffly beaten egg white**
- **2 packages refrigerated crescent rolls (16 rolls)**
- **1 cup sifted powdered sugar Milk**

Stir together first 4 ingredients. Fold in egg white. Unroll the two packages of rolls and separate into 8 rectangles; spread each with some of the poppy seed filling. Roll up jelly-roll fashion, starting with narrow end. Place rolls lengthwise in greased 8½x4½x2½-inch loaf pan, making 2 layers of 4 rolls each. Bake at 375° for 15 minutes; cover with foil to prevent overbrowning. Bake 20 minutes longer. Cool in pan about 5 minutes; remove from pan. Cool. Combine powdered sugar and enough milk (about 1 tablespoon) to make of drizzling consistency. Drizzle over loaf.

Mincemeat Crescents

- **⅓ cup prepared mincemeat**
- **¼ cup finely chopped walnuts**
- **2 tablespoons chopped maraschino cherries**
- **¼ teaspoon grated lemon peel**
- **1 teaspoon lemon juice**
- **1 package refrigerated crescent rolls (8 rolls)**
- **½ cup sifted powdered sugar**
- **¼ teaspoon vanilla Milk**

Stir together mincemeat, *2 tablespoons* of the nuts, chopped maraschino cherries, lemon peel, and lemon juice. Unroll crescent rolls and separate. Spread a scant tablespoon of the mincemeat mixture on each crescent. Roll up dough, starting with wide end. Place on ungreased baking sheet, point side down. Bake at 350° for 12 to 15 minutes. Combine powdered sugar, vanilla, and enough milk (about 1½ teaspoons) to make of spreading consistency. Spread over crescent rolls; sprinkle with remaining nuts. Serve warm. Makes 8 rolls.

Almond Pinwheels

1 package refrigerated
  crescent rolls (8 rolls)
½ of a 12-ounce can almond
  or poppy seed cake and
  pastry filling
½ cup sifted powdered sugar
⅛ teaspoon almond extract
  Milk

Unroll crescent rolls; *do not* separate dough along perforations. Overlap dough to make a 12x7-inch rectangle. Pinch along overlapping sides and perforations to make smooth. Spread with pastry filling. Roll up jelly-roll fashion starting with narrow end; pinch edge to seal. Place on greased baking sheet. Cut roll into 8 slices, *cutting down just to but not through* the bottom of the roll. Pull slices out alternating to left and right sides. Bake at 375° for 15 to 18 minutes. Combine powdered sugar, extract, and enough milk to make of drizzling consistency. Drizzle over warm coffee cake.

Cheese-Filled Rolls

Unroll 1 package refrigerated crescent rolls (8 rolls) and separate into 2 rectangles; pinch seams to seal. Using one 4-ounce container whipped cream cheese and ¼ cup strawberry jam, spread *half* on each dough rectangle. Sprinkle with ¼ cup chopped toasted almonds. Roll up starting with long side; place seam side down on greased baking sheet. Bake at 375° for 10 to 12 minutes. Cool slightly. Dust with powdered sugar. Cut each roll into 8 slices. Makes 16.

Easy Sweet Rolls

Without unrolling, remove rolls from 1 package refrigerated crescent rolls (8 rolls); cut into 8 slices. Press or roll on lightly floured surface to 3½-inch circle. Transfer to ungreased baking sheet. Using one 5-ounce can lemon pudding (½ cup), spoon about 1 tablespoon pudding in center of each roll. Bake at 375° for 8 to 10 minutes. Cool slightly; spoon a little strawberry jam in center, if desired. Serve warm. Makes 8.

Easy Caraway Rolls

3 tablespoons butter *or* margarine,
  softened
2 tablespoons grated Parmesan
  cheese
1 teaspoon caraway seed
12 brown-and-serve twin dinner
  rolls

Combine butter, cheese, and caraway seed. Separate sections of rolls; spread with butter mixture. Arrange *two* sections in *each* muffin pan. Spread tops with any remaining butter mixture. Bake at 450° for 5 to 7 minutes. Makes 12.

Zippy Cheese Rolls

¼ cup shredded cheese with jalapeno
  pepper (1 ounce)
2 tablespoons mayonnaise *or*
  salad dressing
¼ teaspoon onion powder
6 brown-and-serve twin dinner
  rolls
  Paprika

Combine cheese, mayonnaise, and onion powder. Separate sections of rolls; spread with cheese mixture. Arrange *two* sections in *each* muffin pan. Sprinkle tops with paprika. Bake at 400° about 10 minutes. Serve hot. Makes 6.

Cheesy French Loaves

1 5-ounce jar cheese spread
  with bacon
1 tablespoon butter, softened
1 teaspoon horseradish mustard
  Dash onion powder
  • • •
1 10-ounce package brown-and-serve
  French bread (2 loaves)
1 tablespoon butter *or* margarine,
  melted

Combine cheese spread, 1 tablespoon butter, mustard, and onion powder. Cut each French loaf on the bias into 1 inch slices *cutting to but not through* bottom crust. Spread cheese mixture between slices. Brush loaves with the 1 tablespoon melted butter. Bake on foil-lined baking sheet at 400° for 12 to 15 minutes.

Cheesy Bake-and-Eat Rolls

1 6-ounce roll sharp cheese
    food, chilled
12 brown-and-serve dinner rolls
    Melted butter *or* margarine
    Sesame seed

Slice cheese roll into 24 thin slices. Slice each brown-and-serve roll crosswise into 3 layers. Alternately stack roll layers and cheese slices, using 2 cheese slices per roll. Place rolls in greased muffin pans *or* on a greased baking sheet. Brush tops with melted butter; sprinkle with sesame seed. Bake at 400° for 6 to 8 minutes. Serve hot. Makes 12 rolls.

Raisin Breakfast Wheels

1 4-ounce container whipped
    cream cheese
3 tablespoons butter *or* margarine,
    softened
2 tablespoons orange marmalade
    • • •
16 slices raisin bread
2 tablespoons sugar
½ teaspoon ground cinnamon

Combine cream cheese, *2 tablespoons* of the butter, and orange marmalade. Make four 4-layer sandwiches spreading cream cheese mixture between slices. Cut sandwiches into 3 strips. Coil each strip, cut side up, in muffin pan, curving slightly to fit. Spread remaining softened butter over tops. Combine sugar and cinnamon; sprinkle over tops. Bake at 375° for 10 to 12 minutes. Serve warm. Makes 12.

Bread Kabobs

Combine one 5-ounce jar sharp American cheese spread and 1 tablespoon prepared mustard. Make two 4-layer sandwiches with eight 1-inch thick slices French bread, spreading cheese mixture between slices. Trim crusts from bread, if desired. Cut each layered sandwich into 4 squares. Thread a 4-layered square on each skewer. Toast over medium coals till golden brown, 4 to 5 minutes, turning often. *Or,* bake on foil-lined baking sheet at 475° for 6 to 8 minutes, turning once. Makes 8.

Double Special Loaf

1 loaf unsliced French bread
½ cup butter *or* margarine,
    softened
1 tablespoon snipped parsley
2 teaspoons snipped chives
¼ teaspoon dried tarragon,
    crushed
1 5-ounce jar sharp American cheese
    spread

Make three lengthwise cuts to, but not through, bottom crust of bread. Combine ¼ *cup* of the butter, parsley, chives, and tarragon; mix well. Spread between center cut. Blend remaining butter and cheese spread; spread between outer cuts and over top and sides of the loaf. Wrap in foil leaving top of loaf uncovered. Place on baking sheet. Bake at 350° for 15 to 20 minutes. Slice to serve. Makes 1 loaf.

Texas Mustard Slices

½ cup butter *or* margarine
¼ cup snipped parsley
2 tablespoons prepared mustard
1 tablespoon sesame seed, toasted
1 teaspoon lemon juice
¼ teaspoon onion powder
1 loaf sliced Texas toast*

Soften butter or margarine. Add parsley, mustard, sesame seed, lemon juice, and onion powder; blend well. Spread both sides of bread slices with butter mixture. Arrange on baking sheet. Toast at 325° for 25 to 30 minutes.

Note: Or, slice a loaf of unsliced white bread into 1-inch thick slices.

Blue Cheese Strips

2 frankfurter buns
3 tablespoons crumbled blue cheese
3 tablespoons butter *or* margarine
1 teaspoon poppy seed

Cut buns in fourths lengthwise to make strips. Melt blue cheese with butter. Brush on cut sides of buns with pastry brush. Sprinkle with poppy seed. Place on baking sheet. Bake at 375° about 10 minutes. Serve hot. Makes 8.

A Batch of Favorites

Make up your favorites from these three different quick breads—baking powder-leavened dumplings, made with a thick batter; steam-leavened popovers, made from a thin batter; and French toast, prepared from baked bread.

Dumplings, either main dish or dessert style, are easy to prepare. Drop small mounds of the thick batter atop a boiling liquid to steam and cook. The liquid, usually stewed fruit or stewed meat, on which the dumpling batter is dropped, determines whether the dumplings are served as a main dish or dessert.

The thin batter for popovers forms hollow shells when baked. A perfect popover with a crisp, golden brown shell and tender, moist lining is suitable for filling with a main dish sauce or eating in place of bread.

French toast recipes made simply or elegantly are egg-dipped bread slices sauteed in butter. Vary French toast with raisin bread.

Push dumpling batter from spoon with spatula atop bubbling stew or sweetened fruit. Dip spoon in hot liquid before dropping dumpling each time and batter should slide right off. Leave tightly covered while cooking dumplings—don't lift cover to peek during cooking.

Fluffy Dumplings

Make a stew even better with plain, herb, or sour cream dumplings. The orange variation tastes especially good with a canned peach mixture—

- **1 cup all-purpose flour**
- **2 teaspoons baking powder**
- **½ teaspoon salt**
- **½ cup milk**
- **2 tablespoons cooking oil *or* melted shortening**

In mixing bowl thoroughly stir together the flour, baking powder, and salt. Combine milk and cooking oil; add all at once to dry ingredients, stirring just till moistened. Drop dough from tablespoon in 4 to 6 mounds atop hot, bubbling stew in 3-quart saucepan. Cover tightly; let mixture return to boiling. Reduce heat (don't lift cover); simmer about 15 minutes.

Herb Dumplings: Prepare Fluffy Dumplings as above *except* stir ¼ teaspoon crushed dried oregano, *or* dried tarragon, *or* dried sage in with dry ingredients.

Sour Cream Dumplings: Prepare Fluffy Dumplings as above *except* reduce milk to ⅓ cup. Blend ½ cup dairy sour cream with milk.

Orange Dumplings: Prepare Fluffy Dumplings as above *except* stir 1 teaspoon grated orange peel in with dry ingredients. Substitute ½ cup orange juice for the ½ cup milk.

Easy Dumplings

Make these quick dumplings when you are running out of time; they taste great—

- **⅔ cup milk**
- **2 cups packaged biscuit mix**

In mixing bowl add milk to packaged biscuit mix all at once; stir just till mixture is moistened. Drop from tablespoon in 10 to 12 mounds atop hot, bubbling stew. Cook, uncovered, over low heat about 10 minutes. Cover and cook 10 minutes longer.

Choose your best dessert dishes to serve pretty *Strawberry-Rhubarb Dumplings*. The hot fruit mixture is topped with an orange-sparked dumpling. Can you think of a nicer way of introducing fresh strawberries and rhubarb to the family as the fruits come into season?

Strawberry-Rhubarb Dumplings

In mixing bowl thoroughly stir together 1 cup all-purpose flour, 2 tablespoons sugar, 1½ teaspoons baking powder, and ½ teaspoon salt. Cut in ¼ cup butter *or* margarine till mixture is crumbly. Add ½ cup milk and ½ teaspoon shredded orange peel; stir just till dry ingredients are moistened. Set mixture aside.

In saucepan combine ¾ cup sugar and dash ground cinnamon. Add 3 cups fresh rhubarb cut in 1-inch slices, ½ cup water, and few drops red food coloring. Cook and stir till mixture boils; cook 2 minutes more. Stir in 2 cups sliced fresh strawberries and 1 tablespoon butter *or* margarine. Turn rhubarb-strawberry mixture into an 8x8x2-inch baking dish. Immediately drop dumpling dough in 16 spoonfuls over hot fruit mixture. Sprinkle dumplings with 1 teaspoon sugar. Bake at 400° till dumplings are done, about 25 minutes. Serve warm in individual dessert dishes. Makes 8 servings.

Bohemian Dumpling Rolls

    2 beaten eggs
    ½ cup milk
    2 cups all-purpose flour
    2 teaspoons baking powder
 1½ teaspoons salt
    2 slices white bread, toasted and
       cubed (1½ cups)

Mix eggs and milk. Stir together flour, baking powder, and salt; stir into egg mixture. Stir in bread cubes. Divide dough in half; shape each into a roll about 5½ inches long. Cover with large bowl and let rest 30 minutes.

Fill large saucepan or Dutch oven half full with water; bring to boiling. Reshape dough into rolls so they are not flat; drop into boiling water. Boil, covered, for 15 minutes; turn carefully and boil 15 minutes more. Using large spatula, lift dumplings to platter. Prick each a few times to let steam escape. Cut into ½-inch slices. Makes 6 to 8 servings.

For crispy popovers, prick the tops with a fork a few minutes before removing from oven. This lets the steam escape. Serve popovers hot.

Popovers

These crispy shells make excellent bases for a special meat or seafood sauce and they're delicious to eat by themselves with butter—

　　2 eggs
　　1 cup milk
　　1 cup all-purpose flour
　　½ teaspoon salt
　　1 tablespoon cooking oil

Place eggs in mixing bowl; add milk, flour, and salt. Beat 1½ minutes with electric mixer or rotary beater. Add oil; beat 30 seconds more. Fill 6 to 8 well-greased custard cups half full. Bake at 475° for 15 minutes. Without removing popovers from oven, reduce temperature to 350°; continue baking till popovers are browned and firm, 25 to 30 minutes longer. Prick popovers with fork before removing from oven to let steam escape. (If you like popovers dry and crisp, turn off oven and leave popovers in oven 30 minutes with door ajar.) Serve hot. Makes 6 to 8 popovers.

Whole Wheat Popovers

Whole wheat flour adds a hearty flavor—

　　2 eggs
　　1 cup milk
　　⅔ cup all-purpose flour
　　⅓ cup whole wheat flour
　　½ teaspoon salt
　　1 tablespoon cooking oil
　　Butter *or* margarine

Place eggs in mixing bowl; add milk, both flours, and salt. Beat 1½ minutes with electric mixer or rotary beater. Add oil; beat 30 seconds more. Fill 8 to 10 well-greased popover pans *or* 2½-inch muffin pans half full, using about 3 tablespoons batter for each pan. Bake at 475° for 15 minutes. Without removing popovers from oven, reduce temperature to 350°; continue baking till popovers are browned and firm, 25 to 30 minutes longer. Prick popovers with fork before removing from oven to let steam escape. Serve popovers hot with butter or margarine. Makes 8 to 10.

Bacon Popovers

This popover variation has its own herb butter—

　　4 slices bacon
　　2 eggs
　　1 cup milk
　　1 cup all-purpose flour
　　½ teaspoon salt
　　½ cup butter *or* margarine, softened
　　⅛ teaspoon dried oregano, crushed
　　⅛ teaspoon dried sage, crushed

Cook bacon till crisp; drain, reserving 1 tablespoon bacon drippings. Crumble bacon finely; set aside. Place eggs in mixing bowl; add milk, flour, and salt. Beat 1½ minutes with electric mixer or rotary beater. Add reserved bacon drippings; beat 30 seconds more. Stir in bacon. Fill 6 to 8 well-greased custard cups half full. Bake at 475° for 15 minutes. Without removing popovers from oven, reduce temperature to 350°; continue baking till popovers are browned and firm, 25 to 30 minutes longer. Prick with fork before removing from oven to let steam escape. Cream together butter, oregano, and sage. Pass with popovers. Serve hot. Makes 6 to 8.

Cinnamon-Graham Crackers

See these special crackers on pages 60 and 61—

   2 cups whole wheat flour
   1 cup all-purpose flour
   1 teaspoon baking powder
   ½ teaspoon baking soda
   ½ cup shortening
   ¾ cup packed brown sugar
   ⅓ cup honey
   1 teaspoon vanilla
   ½ cup milk
   3 tablespoons granulated sugar
   1 teaspoon ground cinnamon

Stir together whole wheat flour, all-purpose flour, baking powder, baking soda, and ¼ teaspoon salt. Cream together shortening and brown sugar till light. Beat in honey and vanilla till fluffy. Add flour mixture alternately with milk to creamed mixture, beating well after each addition. Chill dough several hours or overnight. Divide chilled mixture into quarters. On well-floured surface roll each quarter to 15x5-inch rectangle. Cut rectangle crosswise into 6 small rectangles measuring 5x2½ inches. Place on ungreased baking sheet. Mark a line across center of each small rectangle with tines of fork and score a pattern of holes on squares with fork tines. Combine granulated sugar and ground cinnamon; sprinkle over crackers. Bake at 350° for 13 to 15 minutes. Remove from baking sheet immediately. Makes 24.

Company French Toast

   2 beaten eggs
   1 cup orange juice
   10 slices raisin bread
   1½ cups finely crushed vanilla
      wafers (33 wafers) *or* finely
      crushed graham crackers
      (21 crackers)
      Butter *or* margarine
      Maple syrup

Combine beaten eggs and orange juice. Dip bread into egg mixture and then into crumbs, coating both sides. Fry on both sides in 1 tablespoon butter till golden brown. Add additional butter each time more bread is added. Serve with butter and maple syrup. Serves 5.

Use two shallow dishes, one for the egg mixture and one for the dry mixture, in which to dip bread slices when making *Company French Toast*.

Coconut French Toast

   2 beaten eggs
   ½ cup milk
   1 tablespoon sugar
   ⅓ cup cornflake crumbs
   ½ cup cookie coconut *or* finely
      chopped flaked coconut
   6 slices white bread
      Butter *or* margarine
      Pineapple Sauce
      Dairy sour cream

Combine eggs, milk, and sugar; combine cornflake crumbs and coconut. Dip bread into egg mixture, then into coconut mixture, coating both sides. Fry on both sides in butter till lightly browned. Serve hot with Pineapple Sauce. Top with sour cream. Serves 6.

Pineapple Sauce: In small saucepan blend together ¼ cup sugar and 1 tablespoon cornstarch. Stir in one 8-ounce can undrained crushed pineapple (juice pack) and ½ cup orange juice. Cook and stir till bubbly.

Simplify the morning-time breakfast rush by having *Frozen French Toast* on hand in the freezer. Because you have done all the preparation steps when time wasn't so short, you can start the morning off right with a leisurely, hearty breakfast for the family.

Orange French Toast

Orange lovers will want to try this unusual French toast with its own orange syrup—

> 2 eggs
> 1 teaspoon grated orange peel
>   (set aside)
> ⅔ cup orange juice
> ¼ teaspoon salt
> 10 slices French bread
> ⅔ cup fine dry bread crumbs
>   Fat for frying
> 1 cup light corn syrup
> ¼ cup orange juice

In small bowl beat together eggs, ⅔ cup orange juice, and ¼ teaspoon salt. Dip French bread slices into egg mixture and then into dry bread crumbs, coating both sides of bread. Fry on both sides in small amount of hot fat until golden brown. Meanwhile, combine corn syrup, the grated orange peel, and remaining ¼ cup orange juice; simmer about 5 minutes. Serve orange syrup with toast. Makes 5 servings.

Frozen French Toast

A good standby to have ready in the freezer. Even the kids can toast up slices when they want a quick, easy-to-make breakfast—

> 2 eggs
> 1 cup milk
> 1 tablespoon sugar
> ¼ teaspoon salt
> • • •
> 12 slices white bread
>   Butter *or* margarine
>   Maple syrup

Beat together eggs, milk, sugar, and salt. Dip bread in egg mixture, coating both sides. Brown on both sides on hot, greased griddle or skillet. Serve at once or place on baking sheets; freeze. When firm, wrap in foil, using two slices for each package and inserting sheets of waxed paper between slices. Return to freezer immediately. To serve, place bread slice in toaster; toast. Serve with butter and warmed maple syrup. Serve 6.

INDEX